AF473943

Eternal Transience Enlightened Wisdom
Masterpieces of Buddhist Art

如來一相
佛教藝術藏珍

Published for the exhibition *Eternal Transience, Enlightened Wisdom: Masterpieces of Buddhist Art* at the University Museum and Art Gallery, The University of Hong Kong, 17 August–16 October, 2022.

香港大學美術博物館於二零二二年八月十七日至十月十六日舉辦《如來一相：佛教藝術藏珍》專題展覽，特此編撰是書。

CURATORS 策展人
Florian Knothe 羅諾德
Walter Chun Hay Chan 陳俊熙

CATALOGUE 圖錄
Walter Chun Hay Chan 陳俊熙

TRANSLATION AND EDITING 翻譯
Walter Chun Hay Chan 陳俊熙
Christopher Mattison 馬德松

DESIGNER 設計師
Stephy Tsui 徐曉雯

EDITION版次
January 2023 二零二三年一月

ISBN 國際標準書號
978-988-74708-0-9

UNIVERSITY MUSEUM AND ART GALLERY,
THE UNIVERSITY OF HONG KONG
90 Bonham Road, Hong Kong
香港大學美術博物館
香港般咸道九十號

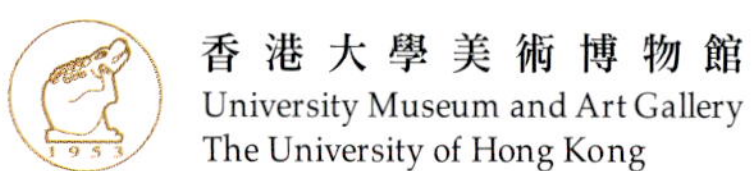

"Tibetans live and die in the certainty that truth is not in things they see, in the things that frighten, trouble, charm or delude them, but just in that nothingness blowing its frosty breath on all worldly phenomena. Asked what is at the bottom of the universal mystery, any Tibetan will answer, the void."

Giuseppe Tucci, *To Lhasa and Beyond*, p. 58

「藏人平生深信真相不在所見、所懼、所惱、所魅、所惑，而在世間諸法所歸——空相。欲知一切奧義，探尋究竟，藏人皆答曰：虛空。」

朱塞佩·圖齊，到拉薩和遠方，頁 58

TABLE OF CONTENTS
目錄

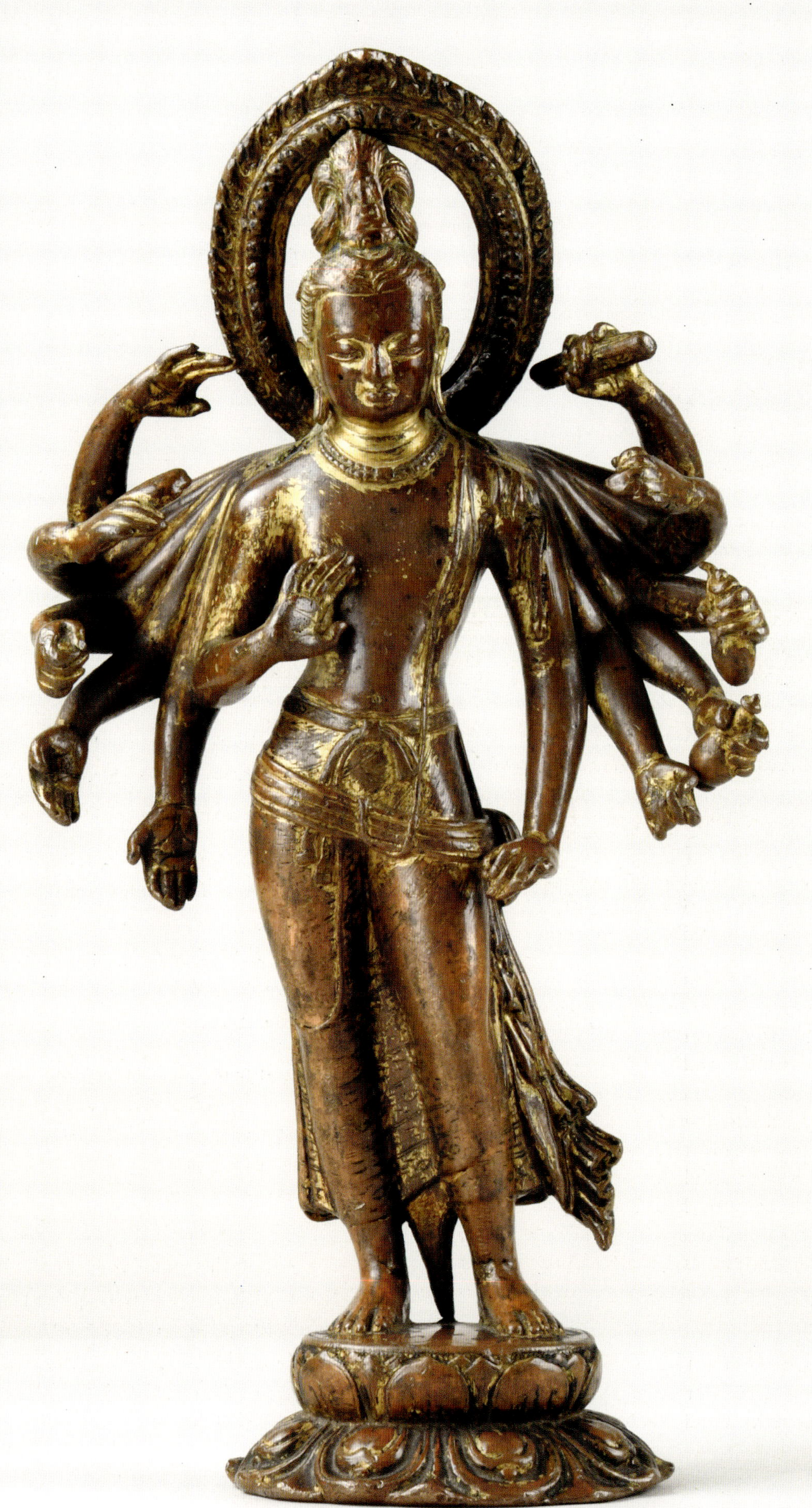

Foreword
前言

Dr Florian Knothe, Director, University Museum and Art Gallery
The University of Hong Kong
羅諾德博士 香港大學美術博物館總監

During the last century, Giuseppe Tucci (1894–1984)—along with other scholars, adventurers and polymaths—researched and published on a wide range of topics that established and expanded the field of Tibetology. Since that time, interest has expanded significantly among new generations of Asian and foreign scholars in both religious and historical studies as Tucci's scholarly findings continue to impact academia and the broader world.

Acknowledging the pioneering scholarship of Tucci and his contemporaries as an academic and cultural reference point, the University Museum and Art Gallery, The University of Hong Kong, worked in collaboration with local collectors to develop the exhibition *Eternal Transience, Enlightened Wisdom: Masterpieces of Buddhist Art* in Fall 2022. With a focus on stylistic characteristics and religious symbolism, the project examined statues and thangkas of deities and gurus from Tibet, Nepal, Pakistan and Mongolia which are representative of Tibetan Buddhist artworks created during the 6th–19th century.

This volume includes a critical essay by Luo Wenhua that discusses the influence of Indian aesthetics on Tibetan art by considering two networks of cultural transmission along the upper Indus and lower Ganges. Following this introductory text, the catalogue section includes entries discussing the exhibited works and explanatory notes on both commonly represented Buddhist deities, as well as on those techniques widely practiced in the making of the artworks. Moreover, the descriptive texts reference examples of the religious symbolism elucidated by the hand gestures, weapons and additional attributes so as to be understood iconographically as symbols of wisdom and compassion.

When viewed from an art historical perspective, these Himalayan masterpieces reflect an array of aesthetic and artistic traditions from neighbouring regions across the

上世紀的學人、探險家、博學家，如朱塞佩·圖齊（1894–1984），研究西藏歷史文化，發表文章，涉獵甚廣，建構現代藏學。圖齊學術成果豐盛，影響深遠，當代宗教歷史研究領域中，藏學逐漸備受東西方學者關注。

承圖齊及諸藏學家之懿範，香港大學美術博物館與本地收藏家，聯袂舉辦「如來一相：佛教藝術藏珍」展覽，時維 2022 年初秋。展出的神祇、上師的造像、唐卡，乃西藏、尼泊爾、巴基斯坦及蒙古 6 至 19 世紀的藝術遺珍，極富地區風格及宗教象徵。

蒙羅文華先生為此冊賜稿，論述印度河上游和恆河下游兩大區域中，印度美學對藏傳佛教藝術的影響。隨之，圖錄部分將詳細探討展品，以圖像學分析宗教符號如手印及法器的象徵意義，後附常見神祇及製作技藝的備註。

佛法從印度傳至喜馬拉雅山脈，及後傳至漢土、東洋。當中歷經王朝更迭，寺廟興衰，僧眾流徙，用以傳法的圖像、器物也隨時地流變。如是觀之，藏傳佛教藝術形相無定，如《金剛經》云：「凡所有相皆是虛妄，若見諸相非相，即見如來。」菩提一相恆無相，展覽故名「如來一相」。從藝術史觀之，源於喜馬拉雅山脈的藏傳佛教藝術，固傳承古印度的美學傳統，並融會鄰近的中亞地區藝術特色，兼收並蓄，自成一脈，其影響更遍及漢土，故圖齊為之深深著迷。

Indian subcontinent and Central Asia. In Buddhism's eternal journey from India to the Himalayas, China and Japan, the religious icons and objects of daily religious practice remain a testament to the shifting cultures that have engaged with Buddhism over the millennia. By focusing on artworks representative of Tibetan Buddhism, this publication and its related exhibition highlight the transitional characteristics of the dynamic religious art of the Himalayas. Through incorporating myriad influences from India, the cradle of Buddhism, these masterpieces formalise a repertoire of deities and symbols that came to dominate Buddhist traditions across China, and which continue to evoke the aura and fascination first experienced by Tucci.

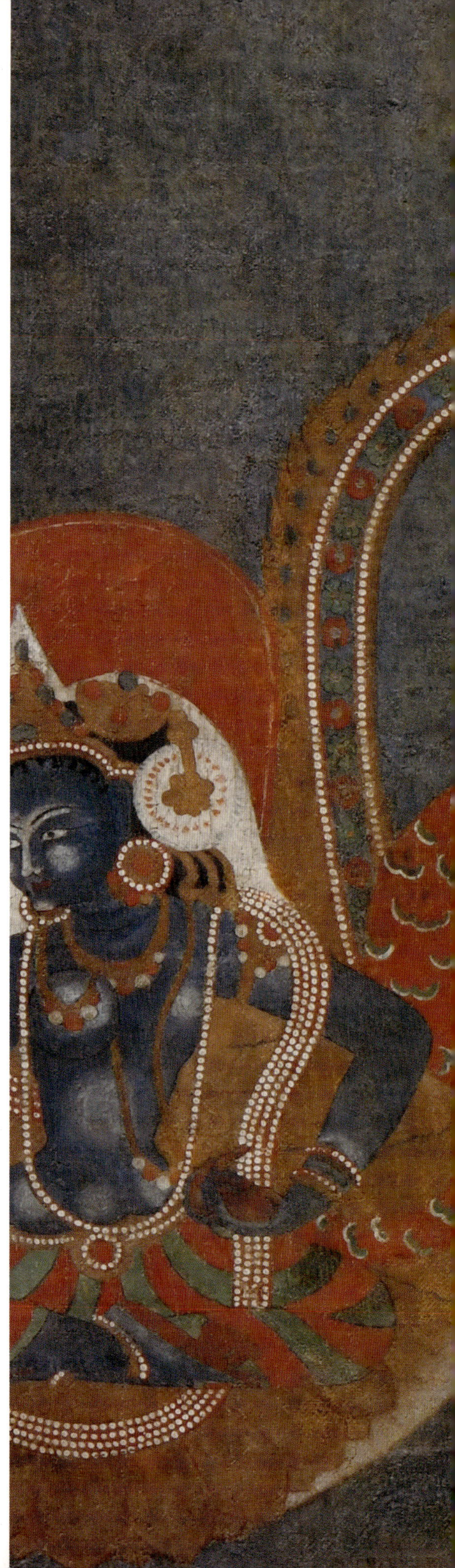

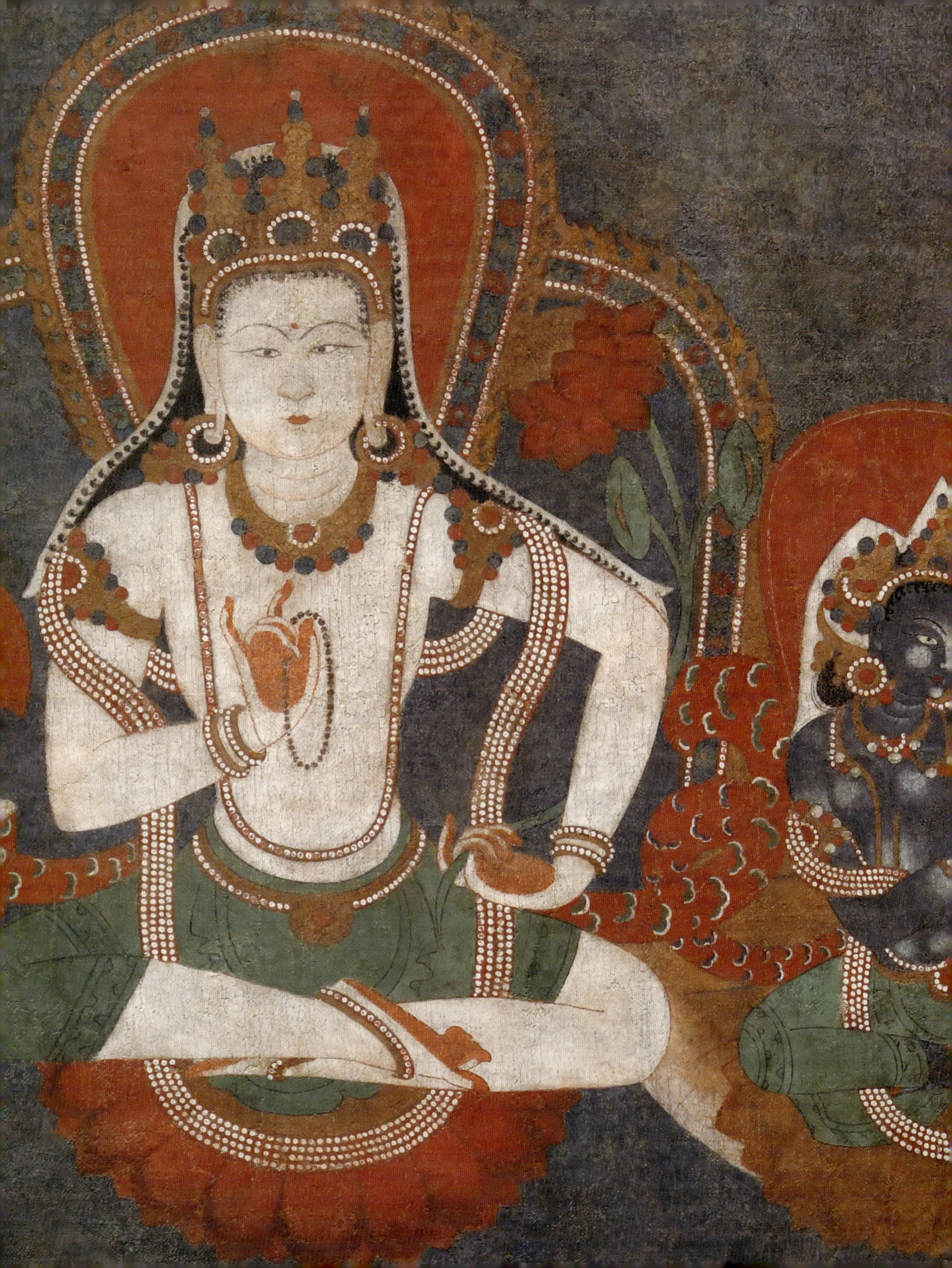

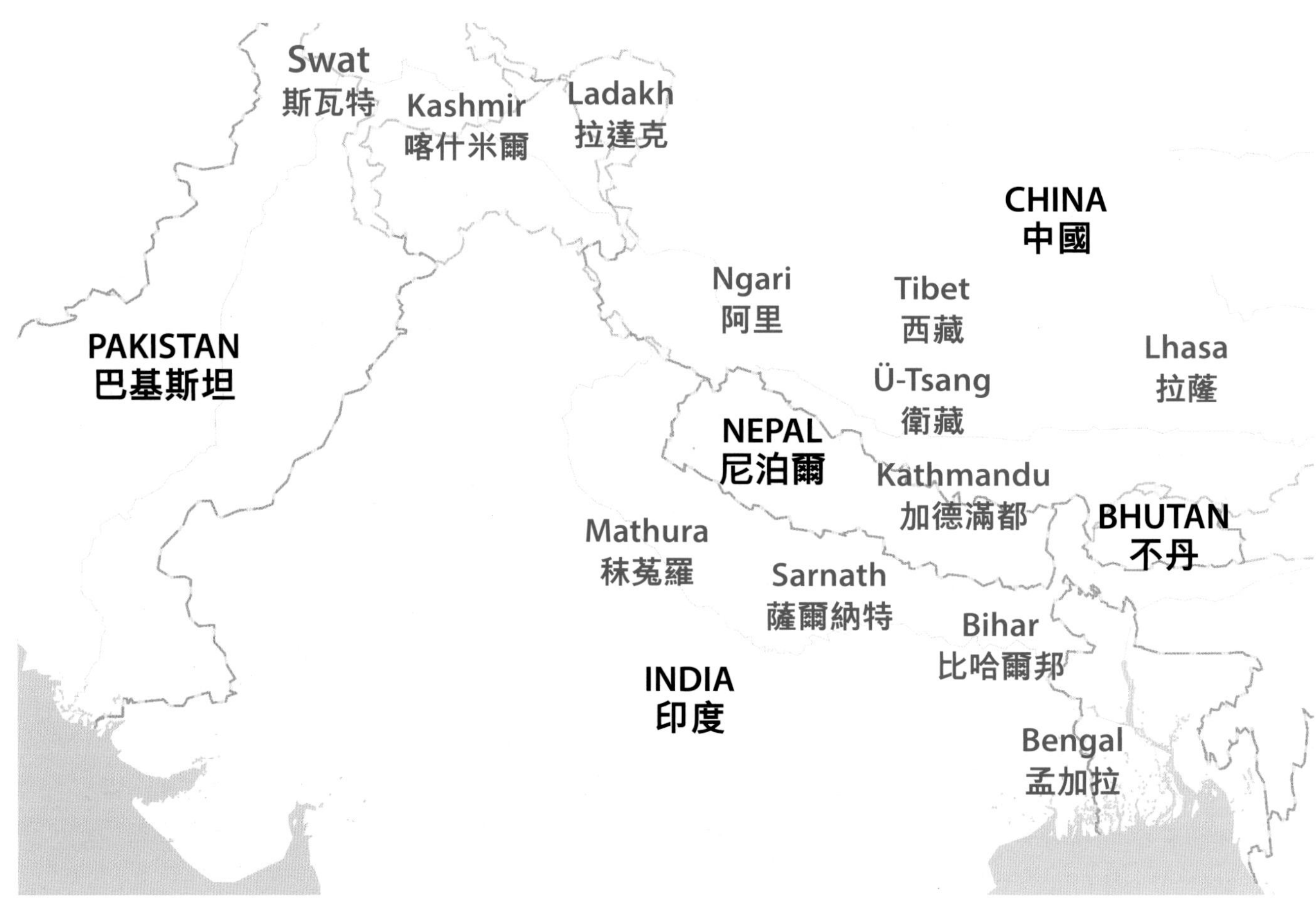

Map of areas surrounding the Himalayas
喜馬拉雅山脈鄰近地區地圖

From the Ganges to the Indus: The Origin of Tibetan Buddhist Art
從恆河到印度河：藏傳佛教藝術之源

Luo Wenhua, Research Fellow and Director of the Research Center
for Tibetan Buddhist Heritage, Palace Museum, Beijing
羅文華 北京故宮博物院研究員、故宮藏傳佛教文物研究所所長

The Tibetan Plateau has long been the epicentre for Tibetan Buddhist art. Spanning 2450 km from east to west, the Himalayan range forms a natural border for China, Pakistan, India, Bhutan and Nepal. Though communication through the Himalayas has always proven difficult, channels of Silk Road culture have managed to weave their way along the gorges and valleys, nurturing the growth of Tibetan Buddhist art.

Ancient India has maintained influence over Tibetan art via two distinct networks. One of these routes stretches from the upper course of the Indus to Western Tibet. The upper Indus region is located in northwestern India and encompasses the art production hubs of Gandhara, Swat and Kashmir. Styles from these regions later spread to areas of the Guge kingdom, including Ladakh, Zanskar and Mnga' ris (Ngari), while distinctive local features also developed in Western Tibet. A second route extended from the middle and lower Ganges to Central Tibet—also known as 'Ü-Tsang'. Located in northeastern India, the middle and lower Ganges included the art centres of Sarnath, Nalanda, Kurkihar and Bengal, which are connected to Central Tibet via the Kathmandu Valley in Nepal and the Himalayan passes. Again, local Ü-Tsang styles developed in tandem with Indian influence.

In this essay I will discuss the development of these two networks in relation to Buddhist statues and paintings, and how the dual routes influenced Tibetan art.

青藏高原是藏傳佛教藝術的中心區域，雄偉的喜馬拉雅山脈位處其南端，東西綿延2450公里，是中國與巴基斯坦、印度、不丹、尼泊爾的天然邊界，文化交流雖受阻礙，但其縱橫的溝壑與河谷像一條條管道，接通青藏高原與絲綢之路，四周的文化得以源源不斷地滋養著西藏佛教藝術的發展。

概言之，古代印度深遠持久地形塑著藏傳佛教藝術，文化傳播的主要路線有二：一是印度河流域上游至西藏西部。該流域位於古代印度西北部，當中包括犍陀羅（Gandhāra）、斯瓦特（Swāt）、喀什米爾（Kaśmīr）等藝術中心，其風格逐漸傳至藏西古格（Guge）王朝境內的拉達克（Ladakh）、桑噶爾（Zangs dkar）和阿里（mNga' ris）等地區，藏西獨特的風格因而形成；一是恆河流域中下游地區至西藏中部（又稱「衛藏」地區）。該流域位處印度東北，當中有薩爾納特（Sārnāth）、那爛陀（Nālandā）、庫爾基哈爾（Kurkihār）、孟加拉（Bengal）等藝術中心，經尼泊爾加德滿都河谷及喜馬拉雅山的裂隙，與西藏中部相連，衛藏風格因而形成。

下文將以造像和繪畫，討論以上兩條路線的藝術發展歷程及其對西藏藝術風格的影響。

Gandhara and Mathura: Art Hubs of the Kushan Empire

Around 45 CE, Kujula Kadphises (ca. 30–80) founded the Kushan empire. The empire's peak occurred in the third century and its area of influence included present-day Tajikistan, the Aral Sea, Afghanistan, northern India and stretches of the Indus. It is widely believed that the first sculpture of the Buddha came from the Kushan empire in the first century.

Located in the area between the Kabul River, northern Pakistan and the Peshawar Valley, Gandhara was a key component of the Kushan empire. This vital hub of Buddhist art was situated at the crossroads of the Silk Road's route to South Asia. With influences from West Asia, India, Greece and the steppes, its art and culture were highly diverse and quite distinct.[1]

The Gandharan style spread throughout the entire Swat Valley, northern India, Kapisa (present-day Bagram, Afghanistan), east of Kabul and Bactria, north of the Hindu Kush and across areas of India, Pakistan and Afghanistan. Thus, it is also commonly referred to as the 'Bactro-Gandhara style'.[2] In Ulrich von Schroeder's two publications on bronze statues, the areas designated as falling within the Gandharan sphere include 'Gandhara, Swat and the Hindu Kush', or as 'greater Gandhara, Swat, the Hindu Kush and the Pamir Mountains'.[3] Instead of a unified style bounded by specific sites, Gandharan art encompasses features of multiple regions.

Gandharan art notably laid a solid foundation for the production of Buddhist statues. From the founding of Buddhism in the late sixth century BCE, no art forms were used to render the Buddha's image, while symbols such as footprints, pedestals, the dharma wheel (*dharma chakra*), bodhi trees and stupas were common prior to the first century CE. The production of Buddhist statues appeared with the development of Mahayana Buddhism. In the Gandhara region, the first known Buddhist statue was produced in the middle of the first century. From the late second century to the first half of the third century, the production of statutes was already well established, having absorbed characteristics from Greek sculpture, such as chiseled facial features and curly hair. Statues produced during this period also featured a crown of

犍陀羅與秣菟羅：貴霜王朝的兩個藝術中心

公元45年左右，丘就卻（Kujūla Kadphises，約30–80年）建立貴霜王朝（Kuṣāṇa empire）。公元3世紀，王朝最為鼎盛，疆域覆蓋今日的塔吉克、鹹海、阿富汗、印度河流域以及印度北部核心地區。

眾所周知，佛陀形象的雕塑出現在公元1世紀的貴霜王朝，其主要藝術中心包括犍陀羅與秣菟羅（Mathurā），兩地藝術風格各異。

犍陀羅大致位於今天巴基斯坦北部喀布爾河至與印度河交匯的白沙瓦（Peshāwar）谷地，屬貴霜王朝的核心地區。犍陀羅扼絲綢之路南亞通道的咽喉，為重要的佛教中心。因屢受西亞、印度、希臘與草原文明的衝擊，當地融會多元的文化與藝術風格，極為獨特。[1]

廣義的犍陀羅風格遍及印度北部的斯瓦特河谷、喀布爾東側的迦畢試（Kapiśa，今阿富汗巴格蘭）以至興都庫什山北邊的巴克特里亞（Bactria，又稱大夏），覆蓋今天印度、巴基斯坦和阿富汗，又稱「大夏－犍陀羅（Bactro-Gandhāra）風格」。[2] 馮·施羅德兩部研究銅造像的巨著，清晰界定了該風格的影響範圍——分別為「犍陀羅、斯瓦特、興都庫什」以及「大犍陀羅、斯瓦特、興都庫什、帕米爾」。[3] 總言之，犍陀羅藝術涵蓋眾多地區，而非特定範圍內、完全統一的風格。

犍陀羅藝術為佛教造像奠定重要基礎。佛教在公元前6世紀末興起後，一直未有直接表現佛陀形象的藝術，僅偶有腳印、寶座、法輪、菩提樹、佛塔等象徵。1世紀後，大乘佛教流行，為佛陀造像奠定了基礎。在犍陀羅地區，現存最早的佛陀像

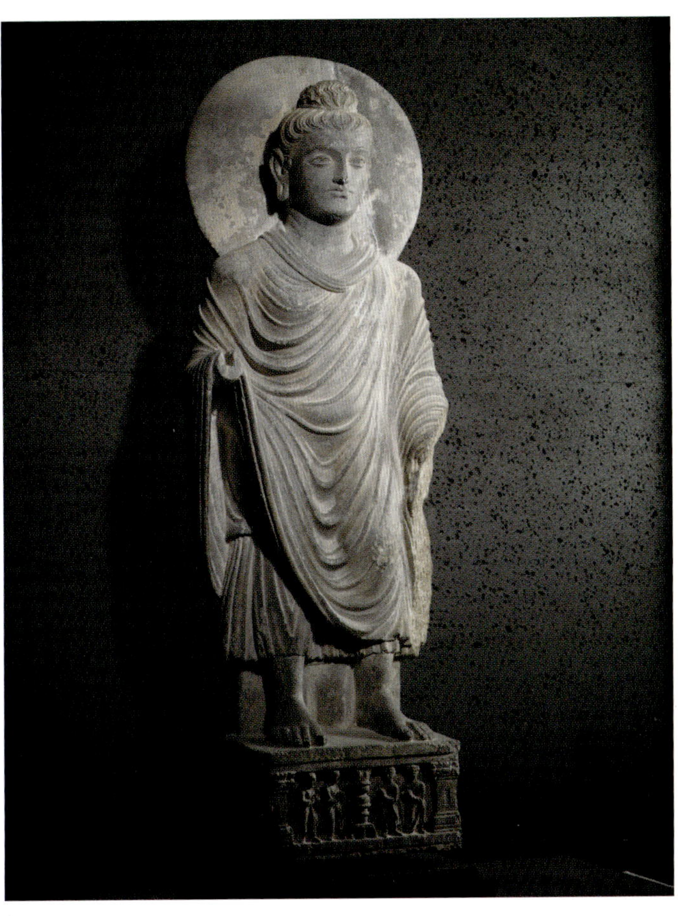

fig 1
圖1

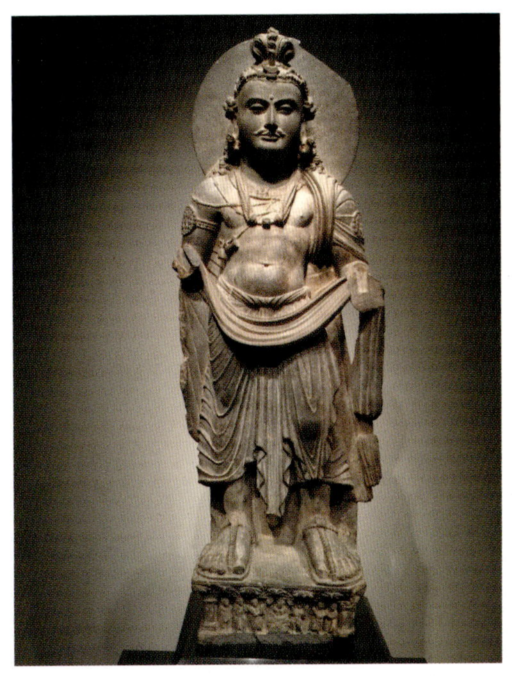

fig 2
圖2

hair (*ushnisha*), were dressed in thick robes covering both shoulders—or only the left side—and were rendered both in seated and standing poses. A standing Buddha (fig. 1) assumes the Wish-fulfillment gesture (*Varada mudra*) with the right hand while the left hand is holding the robe. The statue appears quite athletic and the left knee is bent slightly. Some statues of Maitreya and Prince Siddhartha appear with beards and have elaborate accessories of the nobility, which became the prototype for later statues of bodhisattvas (fig. 2). The most widely used materials for Gandharan statues were schist and limestone, and occasionally terra cotta. Ivory and gold were also used but were extremely rare (fig. 3).

Another major art hub of the Kushan empire was Mathura, the empire's winter palace. On the banks of

約出現於1世紀中葉；2世紀末至3世紀中葉，犍陀羅佛陀造像開始成熟，吸收了不少希臘式雕塑的風格，鼻高眼深，頭髮呈波浪形，頂有肉髻，身披厚重外衣，或通雙肩，或袒右肩，或坐姿，或立姿。立姿佛像右手施與願印，左手握衣角，左膝微曲，體態頗有動感（圖1）。彌勒菩薩或佛陀出家前的悉達多太子像，則佩戴華麗的貴族裝飾，或蓄鬍鬚，為後期菩薩像之原型（圖2）。犍陀羅造像的材質以灰色片巖、石膏居多，陶像（terra cotta）次之，象牙和金像則最為罕見（圖3）。

貴霜藝術另一重心在秣菟羅。秣菟羅為該朝冬宮所在，位於今天印度北方邦（Uttar Pradesh）亞穆納河（Yamunā）右岸、德里（Delhi）東南，據水陸交通之便，自古便是印度南北交通、絲綢之路的要衝。自巽伽王朝（Śunga dynasty，公元前187–前78年）以降，更成為印度的藝術和商貿中

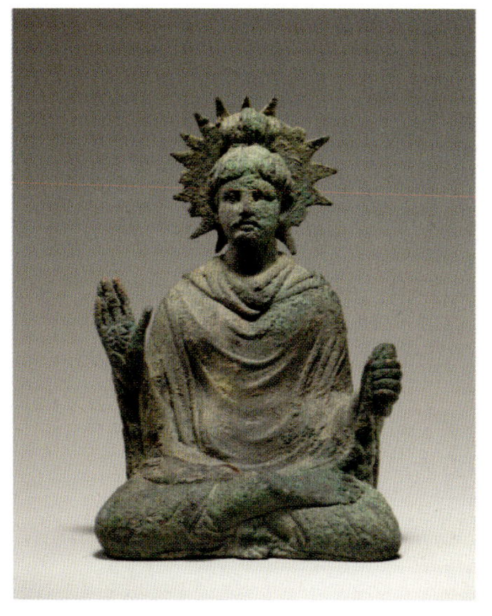

fig 3
圖3

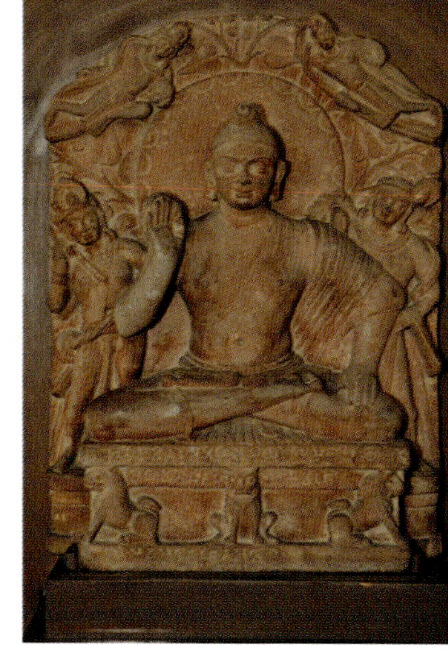

fig 4
圖4

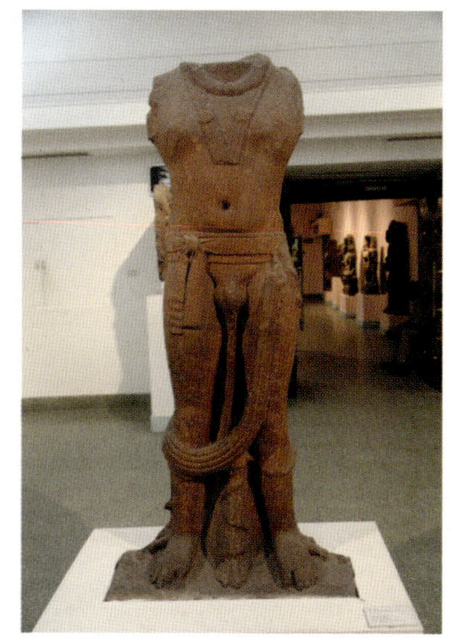

fig 5
圖5

the Yamuna River in Uttar Pradesh, located in northern India and southeast of Delhi, Mathura was a strategic point along the Silk Road due to its convenient overland routes and waterways. From the Shunga dynasty (187 BCE–78 CE), it had been a centre for art, commerce and religion—most notably Hinduism, Buddhism and Jainism.[4] Alongside Gandhara, Mathura was one of the earliest sites to produce statues of the Buddha.

Gandharan statues contain diverse and exotic features, while those from Mathura display local Indian characteristics. The torsos of Mathura Buddha statues are bold and sturdy and the *ushnisha* is often rendered in snail-like curls. The smooth contours of the face allude to the figures' emotions. Another seated Buddha (fig. 4) illustrates the Lotus pose (*Padmasana*) on a square throne. The Buddha is seated upright, with long robes molded to his body. His right hand is raised in the Fearlessness gesture (*Abhaya mudra*) while the left hand rests on a thigh. Meanwhile, the Mathura bodhisattva statue is characterised by an *ushnisha* in short, densely arranged spirals. The semi-naked and dynamic body is heavily ornamented with necklaces and earrings, and a tightly draped wrap accentuates the figure's physique (fig. 5).

心，印度教、佛教和耆那教極為興盛[4]，與犍陀羅齊名，同為最早創造佛陀形象的地區。

相較之下，犍陀羅藝術風格較為多元，充滿異域風情，秣菟羅藝術則呈現印度本土風格，佛陀形像高大魁偉，孔武有力，頭髮如海螺狀捲曲，盤髻於頭上。面部光滑無紋，表情嚴肅，身板挺直，上身穿貼身袈裟，衣紋密集，右手施無畏印，左手支腿上，下身著貼體長裙，於方形臺座上結全跏趺坐（圖4）。菩薩像的髮髻如小水渦狀密集排列，上身袒裸，戴厚重的項鏈、耳環，身體健碩，下身著裙，緊裹雙腿，展現人體輪廓（圖5）。上述兩種藝術風格皆對印度藝術發展影響深遠。

秣菟羅與薩爾納特：笈多藝術的兩個分支

笈多王朝（Gupta dynasty，4–6世紀）約創立於320年。4世紀中至5世紀初，國力、經濟和文化藝術盛極一時，雖只曇花一現，卻是印度史上幅員較廣，最為繁榮的

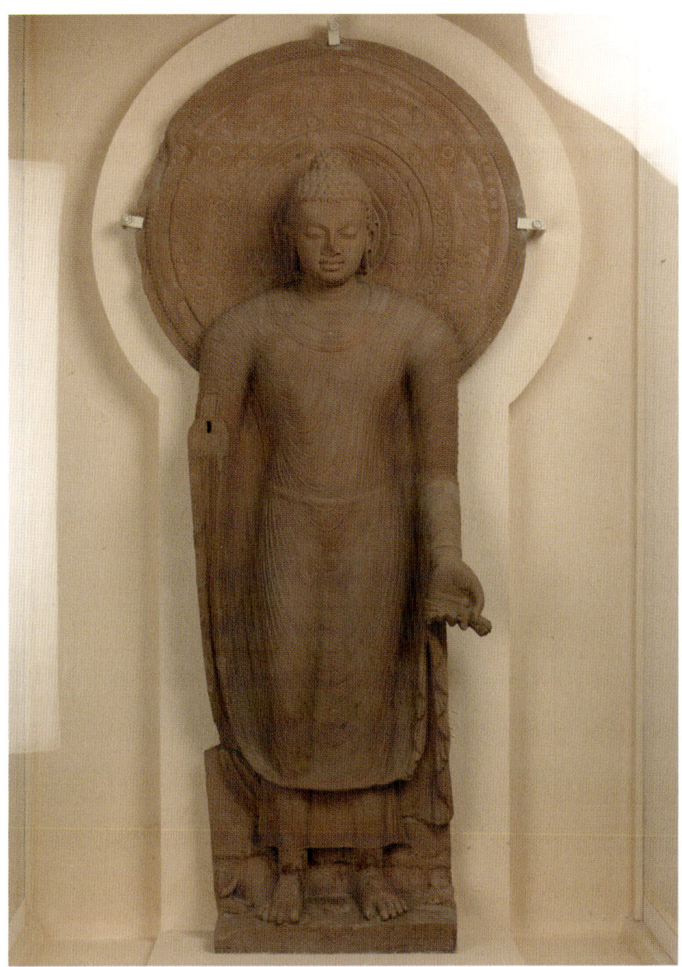

fig 6
圖6

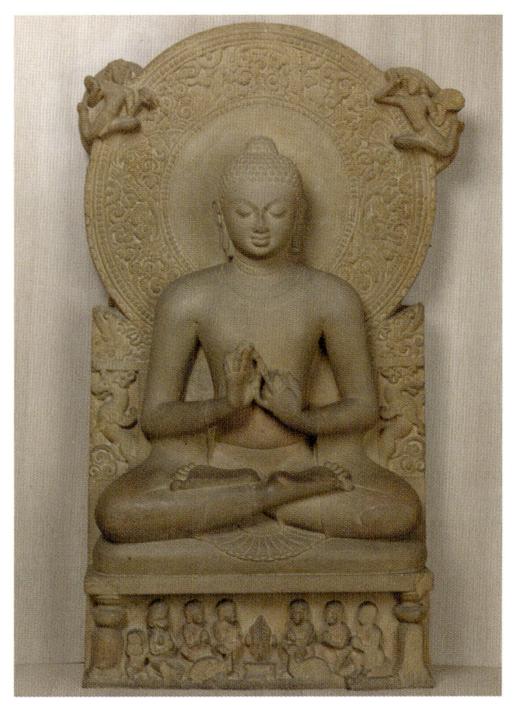

fig 7
圖7

Mathura and Sarnath: Two Branches of Gupta Art

The Gupta dynasty (fourth to sixth century) was founded in ca. 320, reaching its peak in the mid-fourth to early fifth century. Despite its relatively brief period of time, historians refer to it as the 'Golden Age of India', based on its massive territory and remarkable prosperity in terms of economy, culture, art and religion. Having inherited Indian traditions, Gupta art displays local characteristics from literature, music, theatre, sculpture and painting, providing the aesthetic foundations of Indian art. Even after the collapse of the Gupta dynasty, its artistic output remained influential into the seventh century, constituting

大時代，史學界稱之為「印度的黃金時代」(Golden Age of India)。笈多文化承襲印度傳統，在文學、音樂、戲劇、雕塑與繪畫等諸多方面體現本土藝術精神，奠定印度藝術的美學基礎。笈多王朝崩潰後，其藝術風格的影響力一直延續到7世紀，是為「後笈多藝術」(post-Gupta art)。笈多藝術的兩個核心分別為恆河上游的秣菟羅和中游東段的薩爾納特。笈多藝術按照印度傳統的美學，創造出眾多高大精美的佛像，極具代表性(圖6、7)，特點如下：

1. 髮式上，放棄犍陀羅的西方波浪式捲髮和貴霜海螺式光滑髮髻，代之以印度細密螺髮，成為笈多藝術的標志性髮式。

2. 服飾上，摒棄犍陀羅的寬厚袈裟和自然寫實的大衣褶；秣菟羅造像代之

a period of post-Gupta art. Mathura on the upper Ganges, and Sarnath on the east bank of the middle Ganges, were the two primary centres of Gupta art where numerous massive and refined statues of the Buddha were produced (figs. 6 and 7). Their principal features are as follows:

1. The coiffure is fashioned in typical Gupta-styled tiers, with short spirals rather than the wave-like or snail-like curls of Gandhara and Kushan.

2. The thick heavy robes and realistic drapery of Gandharan statues have been abandoned. Mathura garments are arranged in densely ribbed folds, while those from Sarnath do not include any folds. Robes cover both shoulders instead of exposing one, as on the Kushan statues.

3. Robes are closely moulded to the body, accentuating muscularity, especially the legs. Contours of the face are smooth and fine with lowered eyelids. With their elongated bodies, the statues illustrate the ideal aesthetic proportions. Facial expressions impart a solemn air of deep meditation. Where Mathura Buddha statues appear to be middle-aged men with a higher *ushnisha*, solemn facial features and a sturdy physique, Sarnath figures appear much younger, with a shorter *ushnisha*, youthful facial features and a slender, less muscular torso.

4. Round halos are exquisitely ornamented in the classical style, with a mixed motif of petals, floral patterns and pendants, while the edge is decorated with shells. From the late fifth to sixth century, more bodhisattva statues were crafted with sophisticated hairstyles and elaborate adornments. Their elongated bodies incline slightly forward with downcast eyes that impart a meditative state. Influences of Hindu art are demonstrated by the sash and jewelled chain draped over the left shoulder, with legs wrapped in a short, thin garment and a bundle of silk wrapping at the thighs.[5]

Gupta statues were primarily crafted from stone: Mathura school statues were made from red sandstone and Sarnath statues from light yellow sandstone. The quantity of bronze statues drastically increased (fig. 8), while terracotta was popular for making ornaments in

以規律的細密棱條衣褶，而薩爾納特則完全不表現衣褶。袒裸單肩的貴霜樣式不再流行，改以著通肩式袈裟為主。

3. 袈裟緊貼身體，顯現上身富張力的肌肉線條，雙腿圓潤，額部、面龐光滑，眼簾低垂，身材修長。造像結構既展現理想的人體美學，表情亦沉靜安詳，作冥想狀，散發靈光。相較之下，秣菟羅佛像肉髻較高，表情莊重，身體壯碩，現中年男子相；薩迦納特佛像肉髻較低，面龐青稚，身材纖細，肌肉柔和，似青年男子相；

4. 頭光呈圓形，裝飾紋樣包括各式花瓣、花鬘和珠鬘，以貝殼作邊紋，精緻優雅，富古典主義藝術特色。5世紀末至6世紀菩薩造像日漸增多，髮髻變化繁複，裝飾富麗，身材修長，像身略為前傾，垂目而視，氣質安祥，披聖索或絡腋，著薄短裙，緊貼雙腿，胯部繫粗大束帛，可見印度教藝術影響。[5]

笈多時期的印度造像用料以石材居多，其中秣菟羅以紅色砂巖為主，薩爾納特則以淺黃色砂巖為主。此時銅造像數量明顯增加（圖8），陶像則已遍及西北印度至孟加拉一帶，多見於寺廟與佛塔裝飾。

後來，笈多藝術薩爾納特風格傳到尼泊爾加德滿都河谷，對尼泊爾藝術影響深遠。

3世紀後，西北印度的犍陀羅藝術逐漸向阿富汗東部轉移，5世紀時，貴霜王朝瓦解，犍陀羅藝術衰落，但在阿富汗仍發展蓬勃，直到7世紀。此時石膏和陶製造像數量大增，因原料便宜，且材質易塑，利於藝匠創作，故大為流行，多見於佛塔上的裝飾和尊像塑造。哈達（Hadda）、迦畢試、巴米揚（Bāmiyān）、艾那克

temples and stupas in northwestern India and Bengal. The Gupta Sarnath school later influenced local art production in the Kathmandu Valley in Nepal.

Beginning in the third century, Gandharan art was transmitted to eastern Afghanistan from northwestern India. Though its overall influence declined in the fifth century, after the fall of the Kushan empire, it continued to flourish in Afghanistan well into the seventh century. Due to their relatively low cost and the plasticity of raw materials during production, limestone and terracotta statues became popular, especially as ornaments and figures in stupas, such as those at the sites of Hadda, Kapisa, Bamiyan and Mes Aynak. From the fifth century onwards, Gupta art spread to northwestern India, where locally produced statues began to include Gupta features such as thin, tight garments and hair spirals.

From Northwestern India to the Guge Empire: Swat, Kashmir and the Formation of the Western Tibetan Artistic Style

Located east of Gandhara, Swat and Kashmir developed their own artistic styles beginning in the sixth century. Islam rose across the Arabian peninsula in the following century and Muslim influence reached Central Asia around the late seventh to early eighth century as Muslims invaded via the Kabul Valley and Islamised northern India. Buddhists and Hindus in Afghanistan and along the Indus were purged and religious sites were destroyed.[6] Despite the invasion, Swat and Kashmir stood until the eleventh and fourteenth centuries, based in part on their location in the Swat Valley, situated far from any major commuting routes. Buddhists and artisans fled to these areas where Buddhist culture and art could continue to thrive.

Swat, previously known as 'Udyana', produced a significant number of brass statues. Despite their thick garments, for which Gandharan statues are known, Swat statues display many features of the Gupta school, including spiraled hair and V-necked robes draped over muscles with regularly arranged folds (fig. 9). Among early Swat statues, petals of the lotus throne extend down and touch the ground. Double lotus thrones appeared

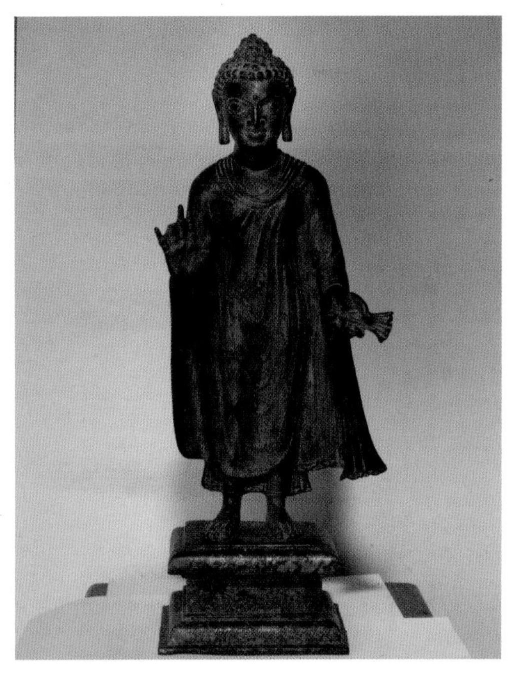

fig 8
圖8

(Mes Aynak)等遺址均有大量泥塑和陶製佛教造像。5世紀初，笈多藝術逐漸傳至西北印度地區，當地造像出現薄衣貼體、螺髮等笈多造像特徵。

從西北印度到古格王國：斯瓦特、喀什米爾與西藏西部藝術成形

斯瓦特、喀什米爾位於犍陀羅地區以東，6世紀以後，當地藝術風格逐漸發展起來。7世紀初，伊斯蘭教在阿拉伯半島興起，7世紀末至8世紀初穆斯林勢力遍及中亞地區，進入喀布爾河谷，繼而入侵印度北部，並將之伊斯蘭化。從阿富汗到印度河流域，佛教和印度教徒遭受迫害，佛教寺塔被毀。[6]斯瓦特處於斯瓦特河谷中，喀什米爾則位於印度河支流的河谷中，均遠離交通要道，地理位置相對偏僻。故此，兩地分別到11及14世紀方告陷落。此前，避難的佛教徒、藝匠紛紛遷至

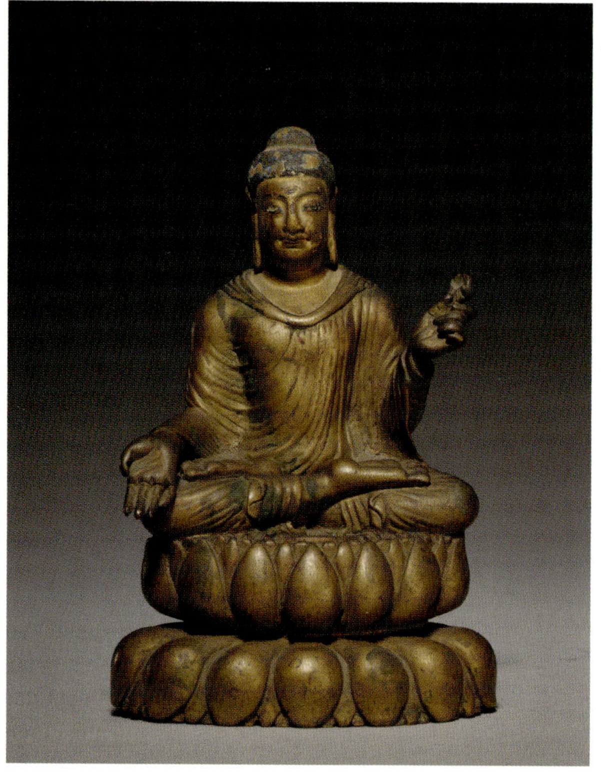

fig 9
圖9

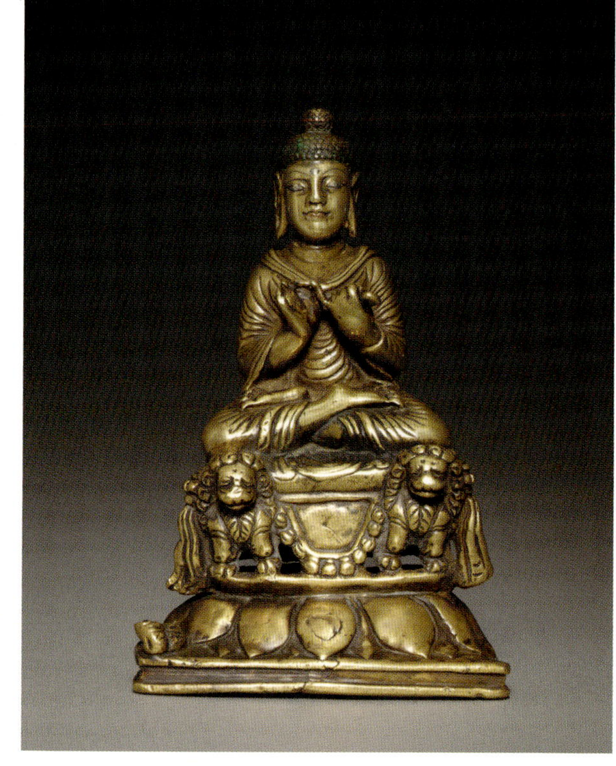

fig 10
圖10

in later designs that are level with the platform. Various combinations also appear, including stone and square seats with animal motifs and an overhanging drapery decorated with pendants along its edge and animals on both sides. The animals are often lions, along with peacocks and elephants (fig. 10). In response to the aesthetics of the Mahayana and Vajrayana schools, statues of the Buddha and bodhisattvas became more heavily ornamented. In general, features of Swat brass statues are highly localised: plump faces have wide eyes and flat nostrils; muscular and dynamic physiques are accentuated by ornamentation in gold, silver and copper for the eyes, lips and the circular dot on the forehead (*urna*).[7]

Swat contributed enormously to the development of Tibetan Buddhism. The Second Buddha, Padmasambhava (ca. eighth century), said to be the Prince of Udyana, was invited by Emperor Khri Srong lde brtsan (742–800) to Tibet. He founded Bsam yas dgon, Tibet's first monastery, and performed tonsure for local novice monks. Buddhism

兩地，佛教文化與藝術得以在兩地繼續繁榮發展，實屬難得。

斯瓦特古稱「烏仗那」(Udyana)，黃銅造像數量較多，雖然佛身袈裟厚重，反映犍陀羅特色，但不乏笈多藝術特徵，如螺髮和倒三角形衣領，袈裟貼身，肌肉凸現，衣褶線條排列規則(圖9)。斯瓦特的早期造像中，蓮瓣多直接著地，其後的設計則多在複蓮下加上平台，還有山石座和矩形鳥獸座——方台正面垂下一簾，周邊飾以瓔珞，兩角各踞一獸，多為獅子，另見孔雀、大象等(圖10)。另外，受大乘佛教和密教思想影響，佛像、菩薩像上的裝飾日漸繁複。斯瓦特銅造像特點可見於數處：頰頤豐滿，雙目大睜而無神，鼻樑扁平，身體健壯，肌肉剛勁有力，眼眸、嘴唇和白毫多以金、銀、紅銅裝飾，本地色彩強烈。[7]

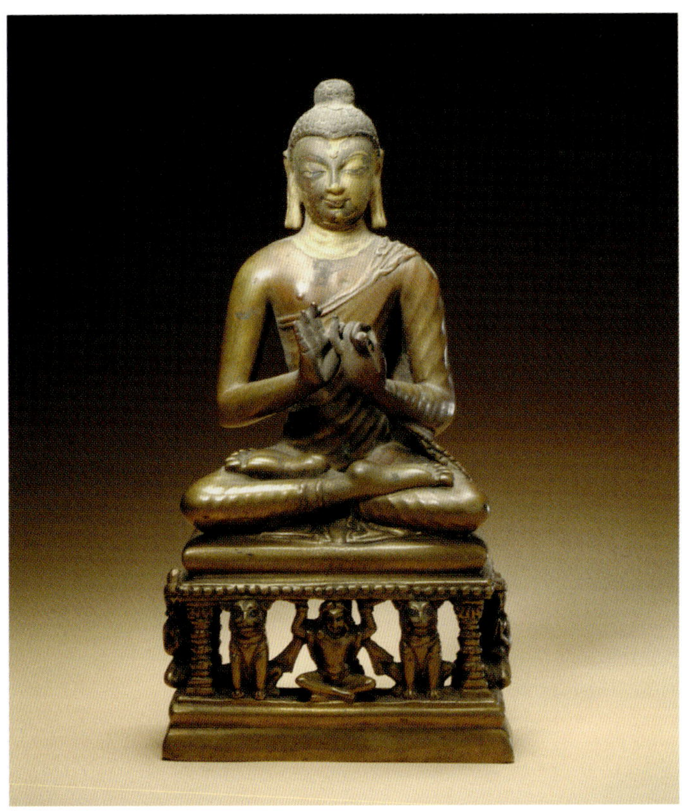

fig 11
圖11

spread quickly in Tibet, with monks brought in from India who were invited by Padmasambhava to teach Tibetans how to translate scripture. Swat eventually fell under foreign conquerors and many sacred objects were transferred to Kashmir, eventually finding their way to Tibetan temples.

Situated in the southeast of Swat and the western Himalayas, Kashmir is almost completely surrounded by mountains. The upper Chenab and Jhelum Rivers, southwest flowing tributaries of the Indus, form a narrow passage out of Kashmir that acted as a natural defensive gateway.[8] A broader definition of Kashmir includes sections of northern India such as Gilgit, a transport hub and sacred Buddhist site that was pivotal for religious art production, despite its relatively remote location.[9] Local monks were known for their devotion, erudition and eloquence. Gilgit hosted the eminent Kanishka Council, also known as the Fourth Buddhist Council.

斯瓦特對藏傳佛教貢獻殊多。據說，譽為藏傳佛教「第二佛」(the Second Buddha)的蓮花生(Padmasaṁbhava，8世紀)是烏仗那國的王子。8世紀，受應藏王赤松德贊(Khri srong lde btsan，742–800年)迎請入藏弘法，於779年創立西藏首座佛教寺院——桑耶寺(bSam yas dgon)，為藏族出家青年剃度，又從印度迎請大德入藏，教導藏族弟子學習譯經，傳播西藏佛教不遺餘力。終於，斯瓦特面臨外敵入侵，情勢危急，許多佛教法物因而流落喀什米爾地區，後來一併轉至西藏寺廟供奉。

古代喀什米爾位處斯瓦特東南、喜馬拉雅山西麓，群山環抱，地勢險峻。印度河的兩條支流——契納布河(Chenab)和傑赫拉姆河(Jhelam)的上游流經此地，為喀什米爾往南、西方向的狹窄通道，加上群山環繞，成為天然關隘，使該地易守難攻。[8]廣義的喀什米爾地區還包括印度北方部分地區，如吉爾吉特(Gilgit)——該區的交通要道和佛教中心。[9]該地位置相對封閉，雖為彈丸之地，卻是歷史悠久的佛教聖地、西北印度的佛教藝術中心，當地僧侶以虔誠、博學、善辯著稱。佛教史上有名的第四次結集——「迦濕彌羅結集」，即在此舉行。後世佛教文獻，皆為之讚嘆憧憬。

犍陀羅藝術衰微後，喀什米爾政治幾經動蕩。7世紀前後，杜爾羅跋·伐爾檀那(Durlabha-vardhana)建立了迦爾郭吒(Kārkoṭa)王朝(約625–855年)。據說，玄奘到喀地時，正值此王當政，在其治下，喀什米爾國土進一步擴張。拉力達迪特亞(Lalitāditya，699–736年)主政時，國力與文化盛極一時。迦爾郭吒王朝歷代國王多信仰婆羅門教，但仍極力維持宗教自由，其國人積累的財富，不少用於建設印度教與佛教(圖11)。[10] 9至13世紀為喀什米爾晚期，國力日漸衰

Kashmir was in political turmoil following the decline of Gandharan art. Around the seventh century, the Karkota dynasty (ca. 625–855) was founded by Durlabhavardhana (r. 598–634). During his reign, the Chinese monk Xuanzang (602–664) was said to have visited Kashmir, from where he reported on the kingdom's greatly expanded territory. Under the rule of Lalitaditya (699–736), the dynasty reached its peak both in terms of power and culture. Despite their belief in Brahmanism, the kings remained open to other religions. Many Hindu and Buddhist constructions were commissioned by its people who had accumulated significant amounts of wealth (fig. 11).[10] Kashmir fell into decline from the ninth to thirteenth century, and was overtaken by the Muslim invasion in the fourteenth century.

Despite continuing some Gandharan features, art from Kashmir was highly localised. Figures featured thin and light robes over well-defined muscles, especially across the chest. Later statues of bodhisattvas included floral or pointed crowns and particularly muscular abdominals. Thrones were designed in the shape of rocks, or with animal motifs, and ornamentation consisted of copper, silver and precious stones for seats, garments and body parts such as eyes, lips and nipples. Statues of deities from the Vajrayana school were also produced within Kashmir, as it was one of the school's centres.

Since the Guge kingdom in Western Tibet was located so near Kashmir, its particular form of Buddhism and religious art were continuously influenced by Kashmir.[11]

From the late sixth to the early eighth century, the Patola Shahi dynasty reigned northern Kashmir, including Gilgit and its surroundings.[12] The dynasty is barely mentioned in history, despite having nine generations of rulers that controlled territory spanning from Gilgit to Chilas. Based on inscriptions that appear on cliffs and bronze statues, scholars have posited that the dynasty had a significant impact on its neighbours in Swat and Kashmir. Local statues commissioned by royalty and nobles were characterised both by their bulk and exquisite nature. In the mid-eighth century, when Tibet conquered Patola Shahi, a number of seized Gilgit statues confirmed that the dynasty's artworks maintained many of the artistic features from Kashmir (fig. 13).

弱。14世紀初，王朝終亡於穆斯林軍隊的入侵。

喀什米爾藝術雖保留部分犍陀羅藝術特徵，但本地風格非常明顯：佛像袈裟輕薄，肌肉強勁有力，胸肌尤其飽滿；晚期菩薩像披長花鬘，戴尖頂或花飾寶冠，身材修長，四塊腹肌隆起；坐具設計獨特，見山石座、鳥獸座等；多以紅銅、銀和彩石裝飾坐墊、短裙和身體部位（如眼睛、嘴唇、乳頭等）。另外，作為密教中心之一，喀什米爾的密教尊神造像為數不少（圖12）。

喀什米爾毗鄰西藏西部的古格王國，對10世紀後藏西佛教復興以及佛教藝術風格的發展，影響深遠持久。[11]

6世紀末至8世紀初，缽露羅王朝（Palola Ṣāhi，古稱「勃律」）統治喀什米爾北部，包括吉爾吉特（Gilgit）以及周邊地區。[12]該朝統治者共歷九代，但傳世的歷史甚少，根據推測，其核心轄地大致位於吉爾吉特/ 契拉斯（Chilas）一帶。學者研究摩崖石刻和銅造像的銘文題記，認為該朝勢力應已滲透相鄰的斯瓦特和喀什米爾，當地銅佛造像由王室、貴族發願訂製，以厚重、精美著稱。8世紀中葉，吐蕃征服小勃律，帶走了一批吉爾吉特造像，可見小勃律也應受喀什米爾佛教藝術影響（圖13）。

842年，吐蕃末代贊普（bTsan po）達磨（Dharma）遇刺身亡，後來吐蕃王室後裔吉德尼瑪袞（Skyid lde nyi ma mgon）逃到西藏西部的阿里地區，與當地貴族聯姻，於925年獲取古格－布讓（sPu rangs，今普蘭）的統治權，後將古格納入治下，建立古格王國。尼瑪袞身故後，其三位兒子瓜分領土，長子貝吉袞（dPal gyi mgon）佔據芒域（Mar/ mang yul），後來發展為拉達克王國；次子紮西袞（bKra shis mgon）佔

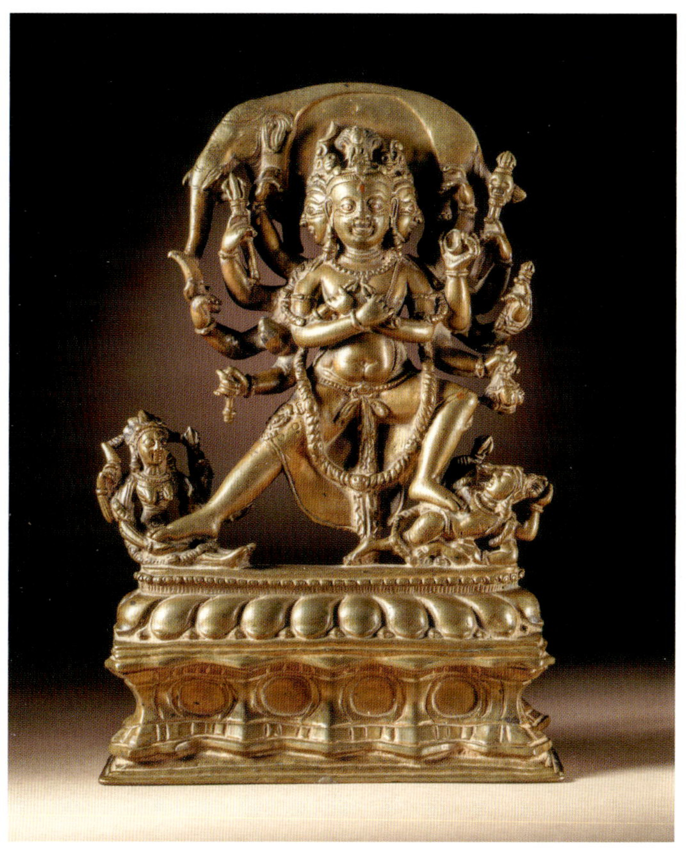

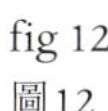

fig 12
圖12

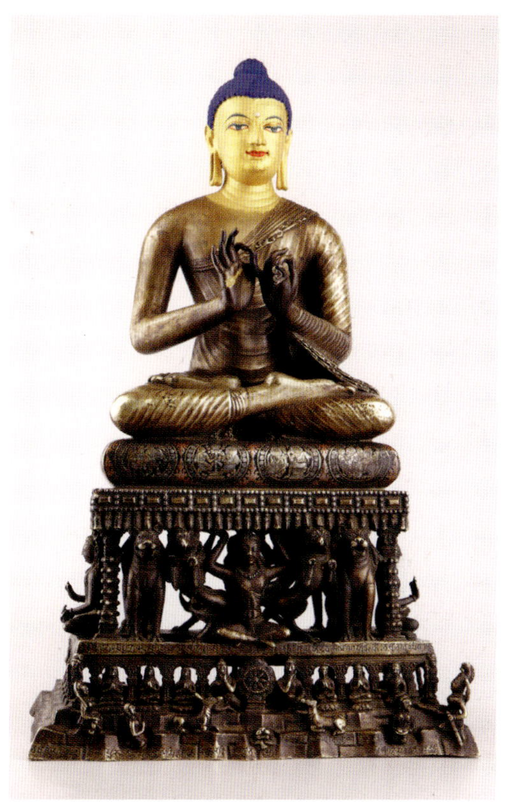

fig 13
圖13

In 842, the last emperor of Tibet, Langdarma (ca. 790–842), was assassinated. Kyide Nyimagon (r. ca. 900–ca. 930), a royal descendant, fled to Mnga' ris and married a local noble. He then gained control of Guge (today known as Burang) and founded the Guge kingdom. After his death, his three sons seized power. His eldest son, Lhachen Palgyigon (ca. 930–ca. 960) founded Maryul, present-day Ladahk. Tashigon, his second son, inherited the Guge kingdom and his youngest son, Detsukgon, ruled Zanskar, an area situated between Kashmir and Ladakh that was eventually annexed by the Guge kingdom. Khor-re, a nephew of Tashigon, played a major role in the propagation of Tibetan Buddhism.[13]

Khor-re (ca. 959–1040), or Yeshe-Ö, his spiritual name, abdicated the throne and became a monk dedicated to the resurgence of Buddhism, thus earning the commendation of 'Lha bla ma', meaning the heavenly or godly lama.

據布讓，控制古格地區，繼承古格王國；幼子德祖袞(lDe gtsug mgon)佔據桑噶爾三個王國，古稱「阿里三圍」(mNga' ris skor gsum)，後逐漸被古格王國吞併。後來，紮西袞的兒子松艾繼承古格王位，以托林寺(mTho lding dgon)為中心，重振佛教，該寺成為佛教復興的基地，是為上路弘法，於藏傳佛教發展佔一席位。[13]

松艾法名耶歇沃(Ye shes 'od)，放棄王位，出家為僧，尊稱「拉喇嘛」(Lha bla ma，即「天喇嘛」、「神喇嘛」)，傾心傾力復興佛教。他派遣仁欽桑波(958—1055年)等21名青年到喀什米爾學習密法。985年，仁欽桑波帶同三十二名工匠返國，開始大興寺廟，翻譯佛典，成為「

Yeshe-Ö sent Rinchen Zangpo (958–1955), along with 21 youths, to Kashmir in pursuit of the knowledge of the Vajrayana school. In 985, Rinchen Zangpo returned with 32 artisans to Guge, where they began constructing temples and translating scripture. He is thus regarded as a leading monk of the Second Dissemination (tenth to twelfth century). In 996, Yeshe-Ö commissioned the construction of Tholing monastery, which was then developed into a hub of Buddhist art and scripture translation. Sometime during the late tenth and early eleventh century, Yeshe-Ö passed away.

During the reign of King Tsede (rTse lde), the grandson of Yeshe-Ö, the 1076 Great Buddhist Council was held, confirming mNga' ris as an important Buddhist centre.[14]

The resurgence of Buddhism coincided with the development of Buddhist art. Artisans brought to Mnga' ris from Kashmir were involved in the construction of local temples and the production of statues. In this way, Kashmiri art laid a foundation for local artistic practices. The royalty were also important facilitators of the resurgence of Buddhism: a bronze Buddha statue in the collection of the Palace Museum is inscribed 'Lha Nagaraja'—the name of one of Yeshe-Ö sons. This and other statues with inscriptions are believed to have been commissioned by Prince Nagaraja (ca. 988–1026), produced locally or in Kashmir, for his private scripture hall, or as part of his early collection.[15]

As Muslims expanded their influence in northwestern India, many monks and artisans were forced to leave. Some were invited to Western Tibet, especially Mnga' ris, along with sacred objects from Swat and Kashmir that would be enshrined in royal temples in Guge, or in other temples in Central Tibet. These objects were major sources for local artisans to imitate. Their skill and ability to integrate the artistic styles of the Upper Indus, especially those of Kashmir, are exemplified by the statues and paintings commissioned by the Guge kingdom from the tenth to thirteenth century at, for instance, Alchi monastery in Ladakh, Tabo monastery (fig. 15) in Zanskar and Piyang Grotto monastery in Mnga' ris.

後弘」（10世紀末到13世紀）初期的僧人領袖，於振興佛教貢獻巨大。996年，耶歇沃修建托林寺，將之建設為矚目的佛教藝術與譯經中心。10世紀末至11世紀初，耶歇沃辭世。

1042年，耶歇沃之子強曲沃（Byang chub 'od）邀請阿底峽（Atīśa，梵文名Dipaṁkaraśrījñāna，982–1054年）住持托林寺。阿底峽大師為孟加拉王族之後，時在摩竭陀地方著名的超巖寺（也稱「超戒寺」、「超行寺」，VikramaśīlaVihāra）任上座，到藏西後，傳法三年，撰《菩提道燈論》（Byang chub lam gyi sgron ma）等著，又與仁欽桑波一起翻譯經典，促進藏西佛教發展。

耶歇沃之孫沃德（rtse lde）在位期間，於1076年舉行了著名的「丙辰法會」，阿里因而成為「後弘」初最重要的佛教中心。[14]

佛教復興帶動佛教藝術發展。仁欽桑波從喀什米爾帶回工匠，參與寺廟建設和尊神繪塑工作，喀地藝術經此直接傳入阿里地區，為當地早期藝術發展奠定基礎。當時王室於佛教復興也功不可沒：故宮博物院一尊銅造像的裝飾佛座前，刻有「Lha Nagaraja」款，正是耶歇沃其中一個兒子之名（圖14）。據推測，該像以至其他有類似題記的造像，由Nagaraja王子從喀什米爾或於藏西本地訂造，為其私人經堂所藏，或為他早期的收藏品。[15]

其時，穆斯林勢力擴張至西北印度，很多僧人、藝匠離開當地寺廟，帶同法器到藏西躲避，而藏西的求法高僧和朝聖者也將斯瓦特和喀什米爾的珍貴法物迎請到阿里，此等法器因此成為古格皇家寺廟頂禮膜拜的聖物，繼而陸續散布到西藏中部各地寺廟之中，其數量題材極豐，足為後代西藏藝匠提供模仿的素材。因長期浸淫於

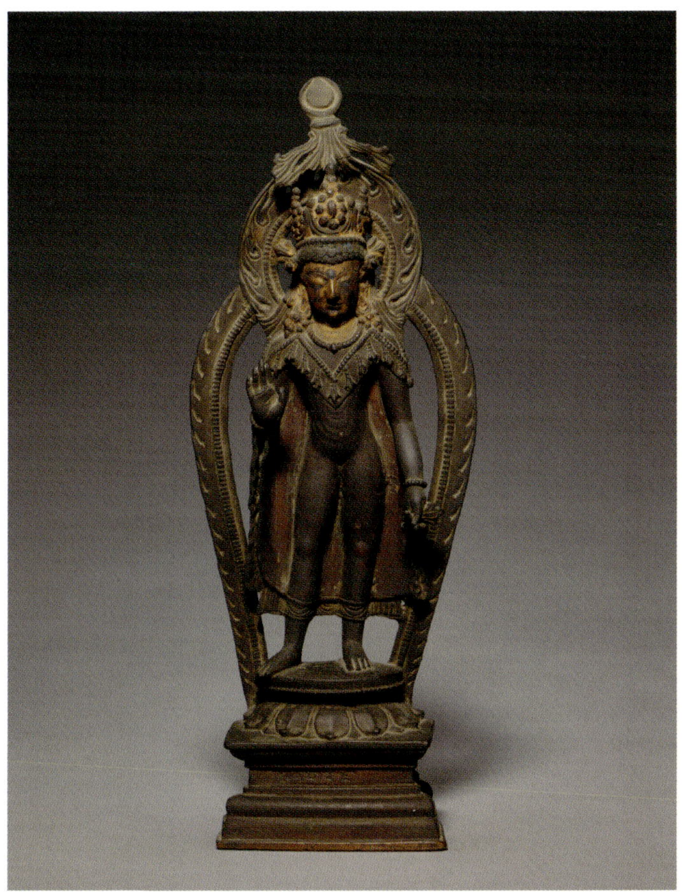

fig 14
圖14

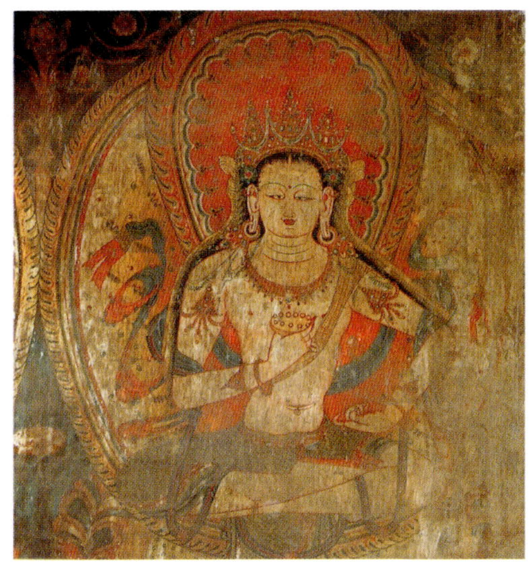

fig 15
圖15

Nemesis of the Holy Land: The Foundation of Artistic Styles in Northeastern India, Nepal and Central Tibet

During the post-Gupta period, Harshavardhana (612–647) unified many of the territories of northern India and brought a brief period of peace and prosperity (fig. 20). However, soon after his death, northern India quickly fell apart. Areas of Bihar and Bengal[16] in northeastern India came under the rule of the Pala and Sena[17] dynasties from the eighth to twelfth century—the last era of prosperity of Buddhism in India, which reached its peak in the Magadha region. Buddhism was eventually driven out from the Ganges by Muslim troops in the twelfth century.

Pala art originated in the Magadha region in southern Bihar, where Buddhism thrived amongst the religious and art hubs of Bodh Gaya, Nalanda and Kurkihar. After

喀什米爾風格，古格王國的繪畫也深得箇中三昧——拉達克的阿齊寺、桑噶爾的塔波寺（圖15）乃至阿里東嘎、皮央石窟寺中10至13世紀壁畫、雕塑，可見古格藝術深受印度河上遊的藝術風格影響，又展示了當地工匠造詣之高，能夠融會貫通。

聖地落日：東北印度、尼泊爾與西藏中部藝術風格的奠基

後笈多時期，戒日王（Harṣavardhana，612–647年）統一印度北部大片疆土，帶來短暫的和平與繁榮（圖20）。戒日王去世後，印度北部陷入分裂。8至12世紀，東北印度的比哈爾（Bihār）和孟加拉地區，[16]受波羅王朝（Pāla dynasty）和犀那王朝（Sena dynasty）[17]統治，佛教進入最後的繁榮時期，尤在摩竭陀地區達到頂峰。12世紀，穆斯林軍隊橫掃恒河流域，佛教被毀。

波羅藝術首先興起於比哈爾南部，即摩竭陀地區，佛教大為興盛，菩提伽耶（Bodh Gaya）、那爛陀、庫爾基哈爾等宗

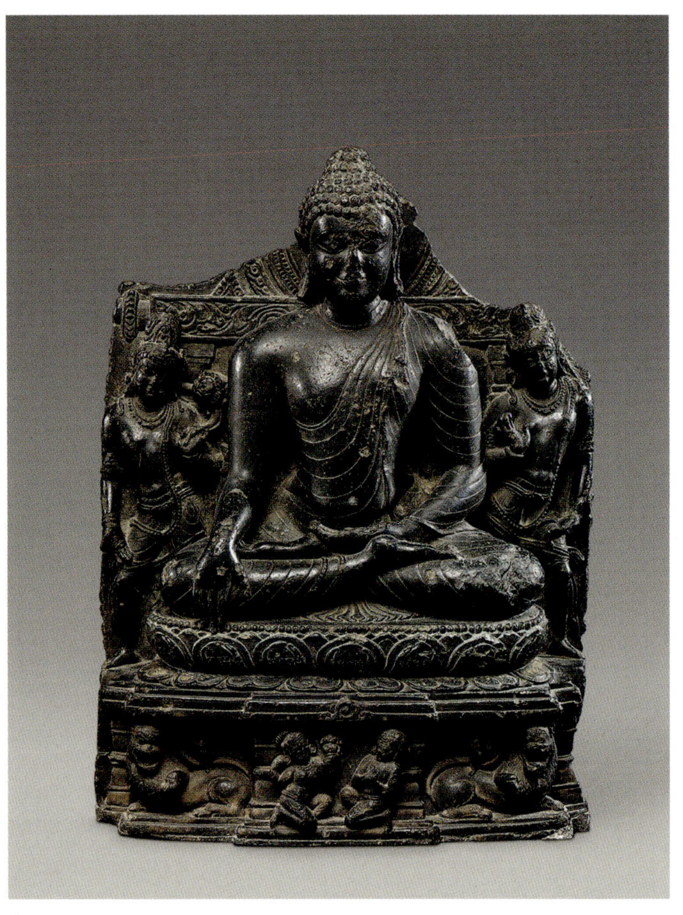

fig 16
圖16

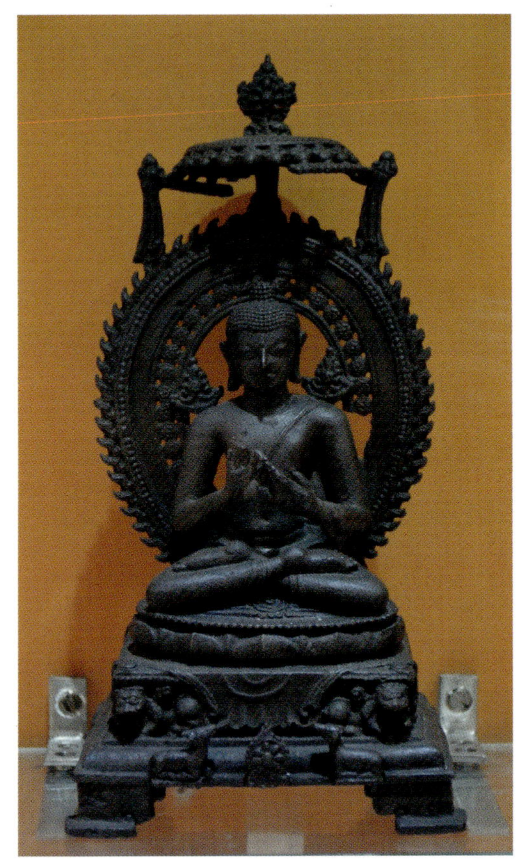

fig 17
圖17

the Sena dynasty overthrew the Pala, the centre of art production shifted to eastern Bihar and Bengal. Black schist and bronze are the predominant materials used for Pala statues. Delicately adorned, the statues, especially those made in fine black schist, demonstrate remarkable craftsmanship (fig. 16). Bronze statues were produced in greater quantity during this era than in the Gupta and post-Gupta period.[18]

From the Gupta up to the tenth century, Buddhism also flourished in Nalanda, an important Buddhist centre in eastern India. It was once visited by the Chinese monk, Xuanzang, whose writings record the scale of the area's architecture and monastic community. Nalanda began to decline after the tenth century and was destroyed by Muslim forces in the twelfth century. Among 51 statues unearthed at Nalanda monastery, 23 date to the early

教與藝術中心分布於此。後來，犀那王朝推翻波羅，藝術生產中心逐漸轉移到比哈爾以東及孟加拉地區。波羅造像以黑片巖和銅為主要物料，黑片巖材質細膩，造像精緻唯美，裝飾繁複，展現極高的工藝水平(圖16)，而銅像相較此前的笈多、後笈多時期，傳世數量甚多。[18]

那爛陀寺是東印度重要的佛教中心，興於笈多時期，到10世紀為止。唐代高僧玄奘曾到此學習，詳細記述了其建築規模及僧人數量。10世紀後，那爛陀寺日漸衰微，12世紀毀於穆斯林軍隊。那爛陀寺出土銅造像共51件，其中23件屬於波羅早期(7至9世紀)，材質以紅銅、青銅及黃銅為

Pala reign (seventh–ninth century). Many were made from copper, bronze and brass (fig. 17), with some gilt (prevalent in Nepal and Tibet but rarely seen in India[19]) and others inlaid with silver, copper, precious stones and glass.

Another site, Kurkihar, 27 kilometres east of Gaya, is located between the Buddhist centres of Gaya and Rajagriha—both pilgrimage routes and art hubs for the production of brass and stone statues. Since 1847, numerous Buddhist statues have been unearthed, with most of them now housed in the Indian Museum in Kolkata. In 1930, 226 bronze objects were discovered beneath a mound (whereas figurines were stored in earthen urns), along with five sacred objects including figures of the Buddha, bodhisattvas, stupas and bells. Among the bronzes, 87 were statues, with 81 of them identified as Buddhist and 6 Hindu. The majority of statues were made from brass, while a few were crafted with gilt copper. Silver and copper inlays are common, along with various precious stones and glass.[20] Most brass statues date from the tenth to twelfth century, subsequent to those of Nalanda. Some of these works are displayed at the Patna Museum (figs. 18 and 19).

Features of Pala statues can be summarised as follows: bulky raw materials, thick and elongated physiques, solemn facial expressions, massive halos and lotus thrones and formal, elaborately inlaid ornaments.

Unfortunately there are no surviving Pala paintings. Scholars can only hypothesise about the features based on miniature illustrations from palm-leaf manuscripts dating to the late Pala dynasty. From the eleventh century, northeastern India was occupied by Muslim forces. As temples, statues and scriptures were under constant threat of destruction, many sacred objects were brought to temples in Nepal and Tibet. Hence, Pala objects became a prototype for local Tibetan artisans.[21] Meanwhile, during the Second Dissemination, pilgrims and learned communities from Central Tibet routinely visited prominent monks and monasteries in northeastern India to acquire Buddhist knowledge, especially from the Vajrayana school. Individuals also translated scripture and commissioned religious instruments that they then brought back to temples in Tibet.

主(圖17),另有紅銅鎏金像,少量錯銀紅銅、寶石和玻璃。紅銅鎏金造像技術流行於尼泊爾和西藏,在印度實屬罕見。[19]

庫爾基哈爾村東距迦耶(Gaya)27公里,位於迦耶和王舍城(Rājagṛha)兩大佛教重鎮之間,是朝聖者必經之地,亦是黃銅和石造像的藝術中心。1847年以來,該遺址先後出土大量佛教造像,多存於加爾各答的印度博物館(Indian Museum, Kolkata)。1930年,該址主要土丘下的一個窖藏出土了226件銅器(小像皆存於土罐內),另有佛、菩薩像和塔、鈴等法器共5件。銅像中87件為造像,有81件屬佛教、6件屬印度教,多數為黃銅,少量紅銅鎏金,普遍採用錯銀紅銅裝飾技術,部分鑲嵌寶石和玻璃。[20]銅像年代多斷為10–12世紀,較那爛陀寺出土者為晚。上述部分造像於帕特納博物館(Patna Museum)展示(圖18、19)。

波羅造像特點總結如下:用料厚重、身體寬厚而略長、表情莊重、背光及蓮座高大、鑲嵌裝飾形式化而精美。

波羅風格繪畫未有傳世,學者只能借助現存波羅王朝晚期貝葉經上的細密畫(miniature)插圖,推測其藝術特點。11世紀以來,東北印度屢受穆斯林軍隊進犯,寺院、造像、經典毀於一旦,大批僧人因而逃往加德滿都河谷避難,無數法器流入尼泊爾和西藏的寺廟,為西藏藝匠提供豐富的素材,波羅藝術因此成為模仿對象。[21]同時,「後弘期」西藏中部的求法者、朝聖者紛紛湧向東北印度,在這片佛教聖地尋訪高僧名寺、求取佛學、修習密法、翻譯經典、訂製法物,並帶回雪域高原,安置於新舊寺廟之中。

受波羅藝術影響,西藏中部逐漸形成其造像風格——背光高大、蓮座寬厚、蓮瓣肥大、身材壯碩、肩寬體

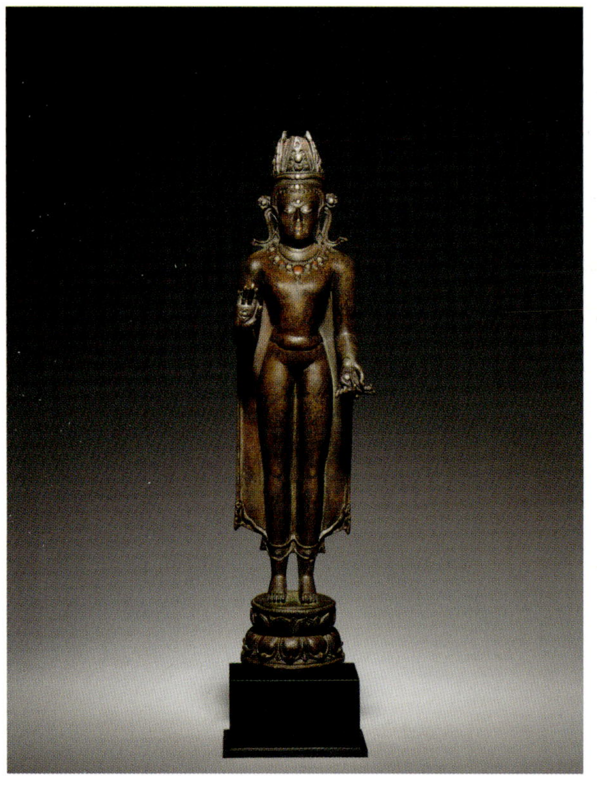

fig 18
圖18

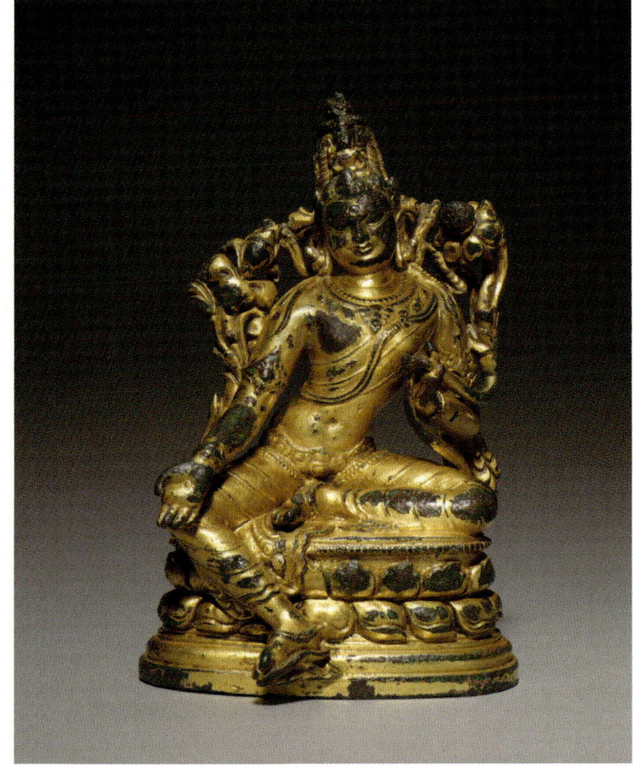

fig 19
圖19

Under the influence of Pala art, a Central Tibetan style gradually developed that featured enormous halos, bulky thrones, thick lotus petals and figures with sturdy physiques, broad shoulders and solemn faces. For example, statues in the Nyethang Drolma temple were primarily made of brass, with silver and copper inlay and precious stones. These statues belong to von Schroeder's so called school (fig. 20). Central Tibetan paintings, such as the murals at the Shalu and Dratang monasteries, display Pala features (fig. 21). As many local Buddhists belonged to the Kadam school founded by Atisha, which adopted Pala artistic styles, Pala painting traditions were seen in the artistic production of later local Tibetan schools such as Drikung and Taklung Kagyu. For example, thangkas produced at Taklung demonstrate the inheritance of Pala art up to the fifteenth century, spreading as far as the Jinsha River.

In the late twelfth and early thirteenth centuries, in the midst of the Muslim invasion, activities related to

厚、表情莊嚴。例如，聶塘卓瑪拉康（sNye thang sGrol ma lha khang）的造像以黃銅為主，有錯銀紅銅，嵌有珠石，神情莊重，身體健碩，馮·施羅德將此類造像歸作不鎏鎦金流派（non-gilt school）（圖20）。繪畫方面，西藏保存了波羅風格，如夏魯寺和紮唐寺11世紀晚期的壁畫，均屬西藏波羅風格代表之作（圖21）。衛藏地區佛教徒多屬阿底峽大師所創之噶當派，該派承襲波羅風格的繪畫藝術，影響後來止貢噶舉派、達壟噶舉派等教派的繪畫傳統，如著名的達壟唐卡正體現了波羅風格的傳承，影響延續到15世紀，直達遙遠的金沙江兩岸。

12世紀末至13世紀初，因穆斯林軍隊入侵，東北印度佛教傳承中斷，尼泊爾逐漸取而代之，對西藏藝術影響漸增。

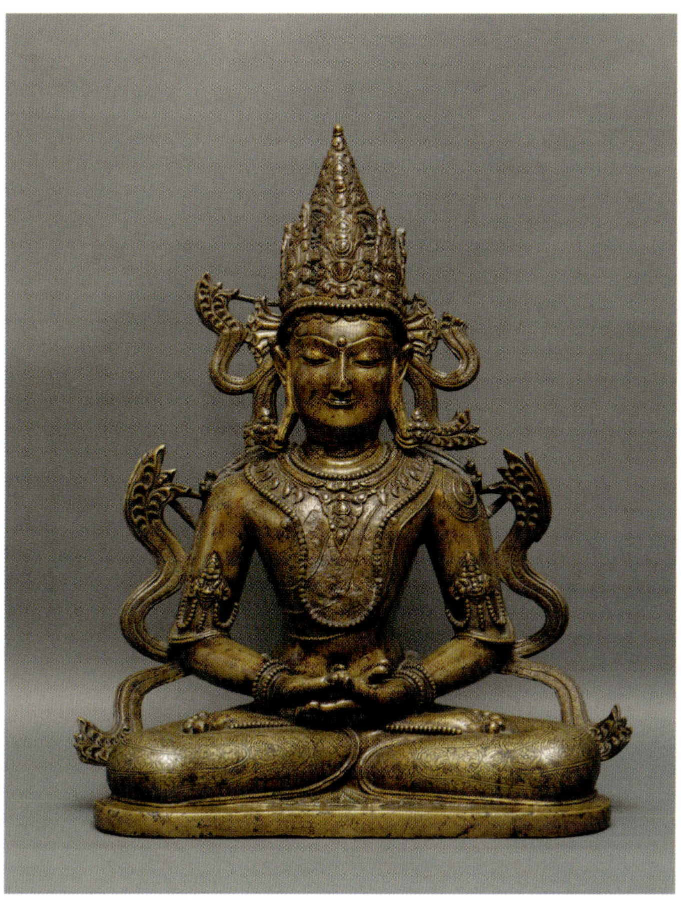

fig 20
圖20

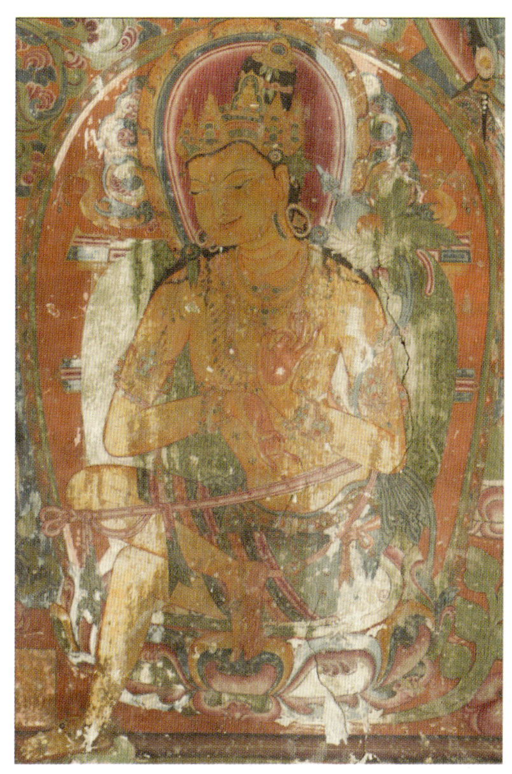

fig 21
圖21

Buddhism ceased in northeastern India and shifted to Nepal, exerting a stronger influence on Tibetan art.

Situated within the Himalayas, Nepal is located near the Tibetan town of Shigatse in the north, Mnga' ris in the northwest and the northeastern Indian states of Uttar Pradesh and Bihar, which heavily influenced its culture, art and religion. Since the seventh century, as transport routes circulated through Tang China, Tibet and Nepal, the transmission of art and culture became increasingly active; in this way art from Nepal became mainstream in Tibet in the fourteenth and fifteenth centuries.

The Newar people in Kathmandu were known for their high level of craftsmanship, architecture and commerce. They produced the majority of religious art objects in the Kathmandu Valley, such as copper statues, wood, ivory and stone sculptures and paintings.

尼泊爾處於喜馬拉雅山脈之中，北接中國西藏的日喀則地區，西北毗鄰阿里地區。其餘邊界均與印度北方邦、比哈爾邦接壤，故文化、藝術、宗教信仰皆深受東北印度影響。此外，7世紀以來，因唐－蕃－尼婆羅（今尼泊爾）間開辟了交通路線，尼泊爾對西藏中部影響漸深，文化藝術傳播源源不絕。14–15世紀，尼泊爾藝術更一度成為西藏地區的主流。

尼泊爾加德滿都的紐瓦爾人以工藝、建築和經商而著名，製作了大部分加德滿都河谷的藝術品，其中多數為宗教藝術品，尤其擅長紅銅造像、木雕、象牙雕刻、石雕、繪畫等。

傳世造像多屬離車毗時期（Licchavi period，500–879年）、過渡時期（transitional period，約880–1200年）和早期末

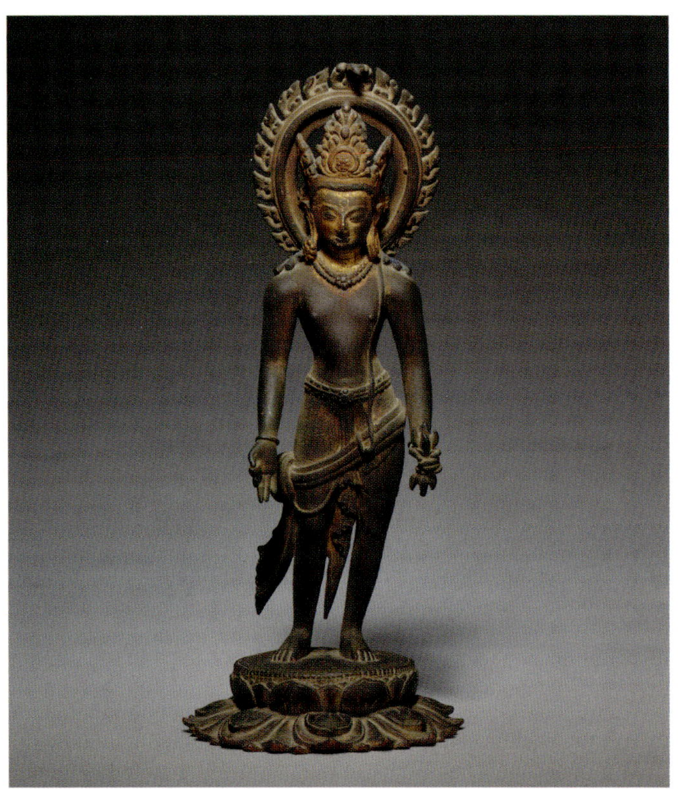

fig 22
圖22

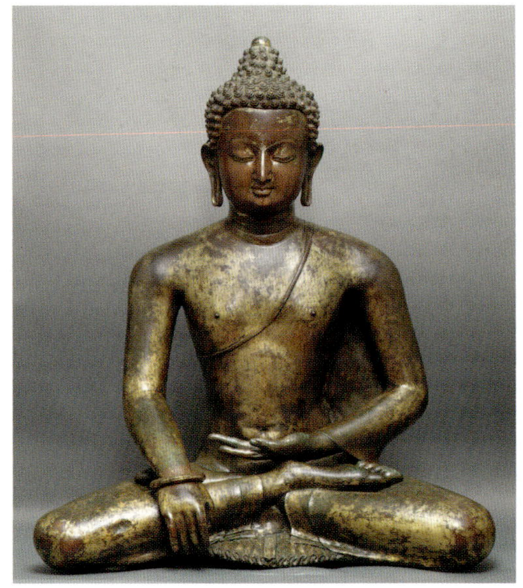

fig 23
圖23

The majority of statues in the region date to the Licchavi period (500–879), the Transitional period (ca. 880–1200) and the early Malla period (ca. 1200–1482). Licchavi art was heavily influenced by the Sarnath school. The majority of statues are made of stone rather than bronze. In general they are bulkier, have a thinner gilt, are rendered upright and incline slightly forward and the outfits are much simpler (fig. 22). The Transitional period was the peak of Buddhism, especially for the Vajrayana school, which was particularly well received in Tibet. Hindu Shaktism had a significant impact on the later Vajrayana school, whose statues were quite different from those originally made in India and Tibet. An increased number of statues and ornaments were seen on stupas, temples, fountains and bronze statues, indicating the wealth of society and the popularity of Buddhism. While few stone statues were produced, the majority were delicate bronze statues with stunning gilding and a shiny surface, which created a calmer overall impression (fig. 23).

羅時期(early Mala period，約1200–1482年)。離車毗藝術深受薩爾納特藝術影響，唯造像以石製居多，銅像較少，體積厚重，鎏金較薄，造型質樸，身體板直而前傾(圖22)；過渡時期為佛教發展頂峰，金剛乘佛教尤其流行，對西藏影響甚深。印度教性力(Shaktism)信仰流行，晚期佛教密宗深受其影響，造像內容異於印度和西藏。過渡時期造像數量增加，佛龕、寺廟、噴泉以及銅造像裝飾繁多，顯示當時社會富裕，施主眾多。此一時期石造像少，而銅造像則精品良多，鎏金明亮，身材勻稱，肌膚光滑，氣質文弱，流露柔媚之美(圖23)。早期末羅時期，加德滿都的藝術水平漸趨下降。末羅人來自尼泊爾東南部的蒂魯特(Tirhut)地區，因受穆斯林軍隊打擊，逃往加德滿都河谷，與當地家族聯姻，落地生根。賈亞斯蒂蒂·馬拉(Jayasthiti Malla，約1382–1422年)在位期間，加強印度教統治和種姓制度，當時尼泊爾文化與藝術最為繁榮。

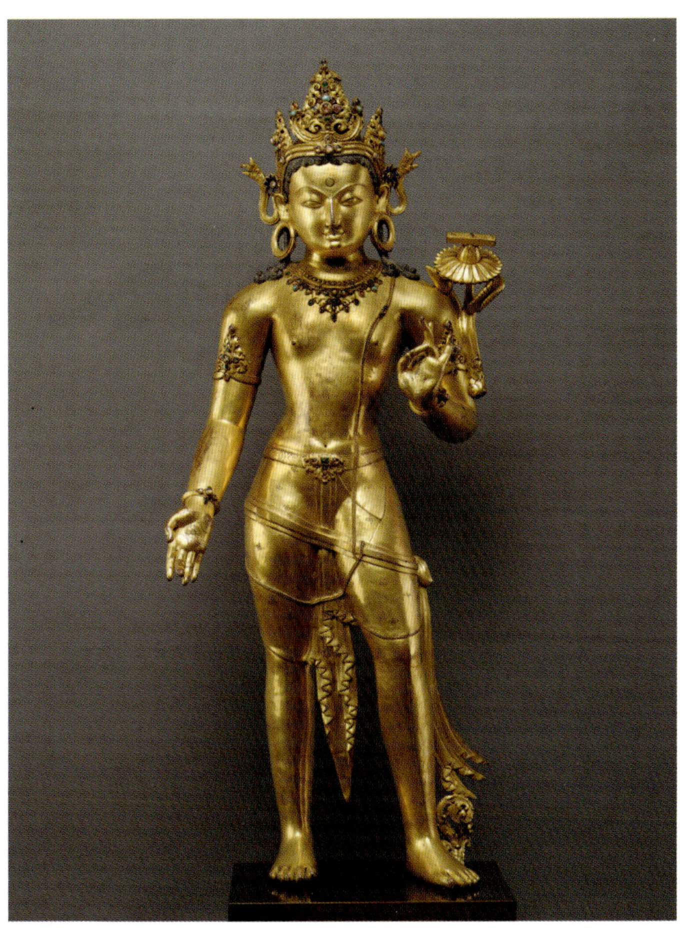

fig 24
圖24

Craftsmanship began to decline in Kathmandu during the Malla period. The Malla people, who originated from the Tirhut region in southeastern Nepal, fled to the Kathmandu Valley due to the Muslim invasion and intermarried with local clans. During the reign of Jayasthiti Malla (ca. 1382–1422), who strengthened Hindu policies and the caste system, culture and art prospered.

In 1244–1349, despite raids from Mathili, southern Nepal and Khasa Malla in western Nepal—as well as continued invasions by Indian Muslims—the economy, art and culture of the Malla dynasty thrived. Statues produced in this period were delicately adorned, with sophisticated motifs appearing on crowns, earrings, jewelled chains and belts, with diverse inlays of ruby, sapphire, glass, pearl and other semi-precious stones and silver (fig. 24).

1244–1349年，末羅王朝雖然屢遭尼泊爾南部馬提利人(Mathili)、西部小王國迦舍末羅王朝(Khasa Malla)掠奪，又被印度穆斯林軍隊入侵，但整體經濟、文化和藝術依然興盛。此時期造像裝飾華麗，尤其寶冠、耳環、瓔珞、腰帶等部分的裝飾紋樣複雜、鑲嵌眾多，包括紅、藍寶石、玻璃、珍珠和各色次寶石，亦常用銀絲作錯嵌裝飾(圖24)。

相較之下，東北印度造像風格對西藏中部的影響主要限於「後弘」初期，尼泊爾造像風格則對藏中影響持久，在14至15世紀達到頂峰，成為藏中藝術風格的主流，15世紀中葉以後，西藏本土的藝術風格方漸成形。

加德滿都河谷一直是西藏與東北印度的交通樞紐，故初期尼泊爾工匠很可能模仿東北印度藝術，而創出尼泊爾本地風格，故西藏藝術風格也受其影響。經紐瓦爾藝術熏陶，西藏藝匠學習紅銅鎏金造像技術，其水平足與紐瓦爾工匠比肩。西藏日喀則市的薩迦寺、夏魯寺和山南市的丹薩替寺的造像，均受早期末羅藝術風格影響(圖25)。[22] 另外，藏族藝匠也創造大量具本地風格和人物特徵的祖師像，甚為寫實，反映祖師的內在精神，是西藏最早的在地藝術創新(圖26)。[23]

早期尼泊爾繪畫極為稀少，傳世者皆屬14世紀以後的作品。雖然如此，尼泊爾傳統的細密畫對西藏藝術風格影響持久，顯而易見。其中14世紀夏魯寺壁畫和15世紀白居寺壁畫(圖27)最具代表性——此等作品均為西藏本地而非尼泊爾畫匠之作。15世紀中期，尼泊爾－西藏繪畫藝術越趨成熟，為其走向漢藏藝術風格，奠下堅實的技術基礎。值得一提，尼泊爾優秀的藝匠阿尼哥(Anige)甚至率領一眾工匠，到西藏及元大都

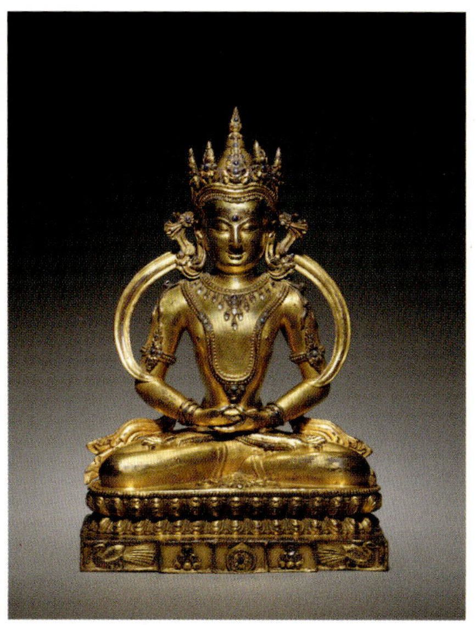

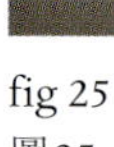

fig 25
圖25

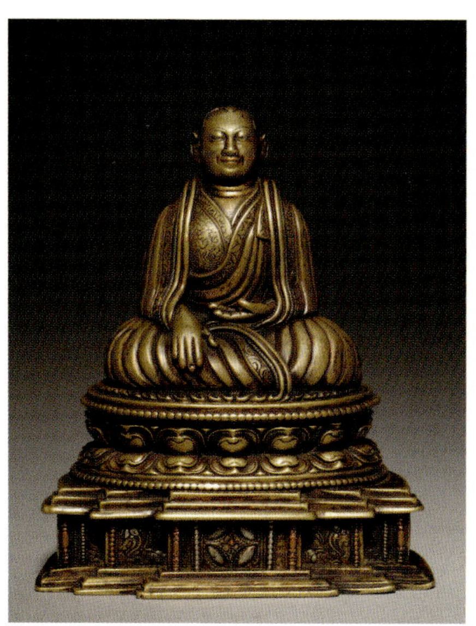

fig 26
圖26

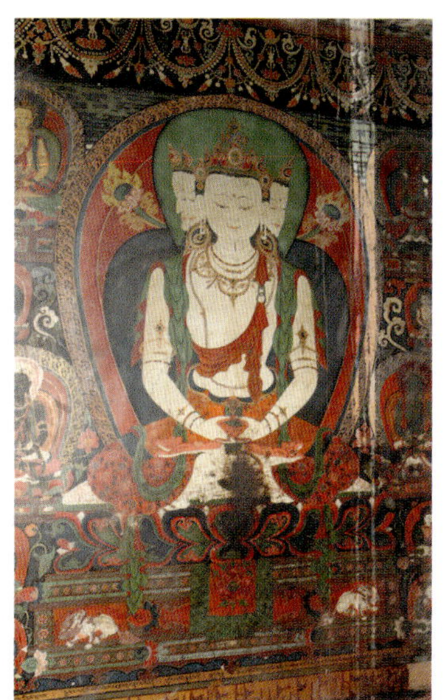

fig 27
圖27

In comparison, the artistic development of Central Tibet followed the style of northeastern India no later than the early decades of the Second Dissemination, while Nepalese influence never completely ceased, reaching its peak in the fourteenth and fifteenth centuries. Only after the mid-fifteenth century were localised Tibetan styles firmly established.

Given that the Kathmandu Valley has always been a nexus between Tibet and northeastern India, it would be expected that Nepalese artisans imitated artistic works from India before developing their own local features. Tibetan art followed this particular route of cultural transmission. Frequent encounters with Newar art familiarised Tibetan artists with gilt copper techniques for statues that were rendered in a style comparable to Newar work. Statues at the Sakya and Shalu monasteries in Shigatse, and Densatil monastery in Lhoka, all display early Malla artistic influence (fig. 25).[22] Tibetan artisans also attempted local variations as they produced numerous realistic statues of the founding masters (of local Buddhist schools), styled with significant local characteristics when portraying human figures (fig. 26).[23]

Very few paintings from Nepal dating from before the fourteenth century have survived. Even so, it is obvious

（今北京）興修佛教建築，尼泊爾藝術因而直達元代宮廷，推動明清漢藏藝術風格發展。

結語

在常見的絲綢之路交通路線圖上，西藏總是空白的——似乎此高原禁區為世所忘。而事實並非如此，史料和文物皆可證明，西藏曾是絲綢之路的重要支線，與周邊地區交流頻繁。藏西藝術即在西北印度藝術的滋養下成長起來。藏中、尼泊爾與東北印度間正是朝聖、求法以及藝術傳播之路，大量珍貴的聖物諸如貝葉經、佛像、唐卡等，從佛陀故土帶到雪域高原的寺廟中，受供奉膜拜，保存至今。如此看來，喜馬拉雅山間的通道就如帶來水源和養分的溪流，曾給青藏高原灌注信仰、文化與藝術，使得平瘠的土地上，開出驚艷的佛教藝術之花。

7世紀時，佛教雖已傳至青藏的四周，但雪域高原仍是佛法的處女地，尚待開墾和

that the miniature illustrations in the Nepalese tradition had a significant impact on Tibetan artistic styles. The murals at the Shalu and Palcho monasteries (fig. 27), dating to the fourteenth and fifteenth centuries, respectively, are typical examples of Tibetan rather than Nepalese painting. The Nepalese-Tibetan artistic tradition had matured by the mid-fifteenth century, laying a solid foundation for its later development towards the Sino-Tibetan style. It is worth mentioning that Araniko (1244–1318), a brilliant Nepalese artisan, was invited to Tibet and Yuan Dadu (present-day Beijing) with his fellow artisans to construct Buddhist forms of architecture. In this way, Nepalese art was directly imported to the Yuan court, promoting Sino-Tibetan artistic development during the Ming and Qing dynasties.

Conclusion

On maps illustrating the Silk Road, Tibet is often left blank and appears to be nearly forgotten. History and artefacts, however, rebut such a misconception, proving that Tibet was once an important route along the Silk Road, and that it interacted closely with neighbouring regions. Art in Western Tibet matured thanks to the rich sources of artwork from northwestern India. Meanwhile, Central Tibet was linked to Nepal and northeastern India by cultural transmission via pilgrimage routes, along which countless precious sacred objects such as palm-leaf manuscripts, Buddha statues and thangkas were brought from the homeland of the Buddha to be worshipped in temples on the plateau.

In the seventh century, Buddhism was still largely unknown on the plateau, though it had spread widely throughout the surrounding regions. By the twelfth to fourteenth century, Buddhism was deeply rooted in Tibet, and a distinct form of Buddhist art had developed into the spiritual world of Tibetans. However, from northwestern to northeastern India, from the South Asian subcontinent to the foot of the Himalayas, the Buddha's halo remained veiled, as the plateau endured as the centre of Buddhism.

播種；時至12–14世紀，佛教已在青藏高原紮根，發展出獨一無二的藏傳佛教藝術，更成為藏族精神世界的象徵，然而從西北到東北印度、從南亞次大陸到喜馬拉雅山，周圍佛國的寶光卻如殘蠋般，一支支被吹滅了，雪域高原更成為佛教的聖地和中心。

Notes 註解

1. 孫英剛、何平：《犍陀羅文明史》（北京：三聯書店，2018年），頁2。Sun, Y.-G. and He, P. *Jiantuoluo Wenming Shi (History of the Gandharan Civilisation)* (Beijing: Sanlian Publication House, 2018), 2.

2. Huntington, S. L., *The Art of Ancient India: Buddhist, Hindu, Jain* (New York: Weather Hill, 2001), 116.

3. Von Schroeder, U., *Indo-Tibetan Bronzes* (Hong Kong: Visual Dharma Publications, 2008), 65–98; von Schroeder, U., *Buddhist Sculptures in Tibet, Volume One: India and Nepal* (Hong Kong: Visual Dharma Publications, 2001), 53–210.

4. Sharma, R. C., *Buddhist Art of Mathura* (Delhi: Agam Kala Prakashan, 1984), 4–7, 27–28; Indian Museum (ed.), *Mathura Sculptures: A Catalogue of Sculptures of Mathura School in the Indian Museum* (Kolkata: Indian Museum, 2006), 2–3.

5. 羅文華：《梵天東土並蒂蓮華：公元400–700年印度與中國雕塑藝術》（北京：故宮出版社，2016年），頁488–498。Luo, W.-H., *Fantian Dongtu Bingdi Lianhua: Gongyuan 400–700 Nian Yindu Yu Zhongguo Diaosu Yishu (Sculptural Art of India and China, 400–700 C.E.)* (Beijing: Forbidden City Publishing House, 2016), 488–498.

6. Singh, U., *A History of Ancient and Early Medieval India: From the Stone Age to the 12th Century* (New Delhi: Pearson, 2008), 572–573.

7. 羅文華：〈故宮博物院藏古印度斯瓦特銅佛像研究——兼論斯瓦特風格的形成〉，《故宮博物院院刊》，1997年第3期，頁84–91。Von Schroeder, Ulrich, *Indo-Tibetan Bronzes*, 82–97, pls. 5A-12H; Buddhist Sculptures in Tibet, 12–51, pls. 2A-11E.

8. Rabbani, G. M., *Kashmir, Social and Cultural History* (Delhi: Anmol Publications, 1986), 44–50.

9. Linrothe, R., *Collecting Paradise: Buddhist Art of Kashmir and its Legacies* (New York: Rubin Museum of Art, 2014), xi.

10. Hassnain, F. M., *Hindu Kashmir* (New Delhi: Light and Life Publishers, 1977), 51–52.

11. 羅文華：〈故宮藏喀什米爾風格銅造像研究〉，《故宮博物院院刊》，2001年第5期，頁63–74。Luo W.-H., 'Gugong Cang Keshimi'er Fengge Tong Zaoxiang Yanjiu (Study on Bronze Figures in Kashmiri Style in the Collection of the Palace Museum)', *Palace Museum Journal*, 5, 2001, 63–74.

12. Von Hinüber, O., *Die Palola Ṣāhis: Ihre Steininschriften, Inschriften auf Bronzen, Handschriftenkolophone und Schutzzauber, Materialien zur Geschichte von Gilgit und Chilas* (Mainz: Zabern, 2004).

13. Von Schroeder, U., *Buddhist Sculptures in Tibet*, 69.

14. 王森：《西藏佛教發展史略》（北京：中國社會科學院出版社，1987年），頁29–34。Wang, S., *Xizang Fojiao Fazhan Shilue (History of Tibetan Buddhism)* (Beijing: China Social Sciences Press, 1987), 29–34.

15. Von Schroeder, Ulrich, *Buddhist Sculptures in Tibet*, 84–86; 羅文華：〈西藏古格那嘎拉咱王及其銅像分析〉，《故宮學術季刊》，1998年第16卷1期，頁183–192。(Luo W.-H., 'A Kashmir Style Buddha Sculpture and the Tibetan Gelun King "Nagaradza"', The National Palace Museum Research Quarterly, 16(1), 1989, 183–192.)

16. Bengal at this time encompassed today's state of West Bengal and Bangladesh. 孟加拉地區包括今天印度的西孟加拉邦和孟加拉國。

17. Its reign spanned from the late 11th to the early 13th century, mainly in Bengal. 11世紀末至13世紀初，主要統治孟加拉地區。

18. Huntington, S. L., *The Art of Ancient India: Buddhist, Hindu, Jain*, 387–388.

19. Paul, D., *The Art of Nalanda: Development of Buddhist Sculpture AD 600–1200* (New Delhi: Munshiram Manoharial Publishers, 1995).

20. Von Schroeder, U., *Indo-Tibetan Bronzes* (Hong Kong: Visual Dharma Publications, 1981), Chapter X-XIII, XVII.

21. Martin, D., "Painters, Patrons and Paintings of Patrons in Early Tibetan Art", in Rob Linrothe and Henrik H. Sørensen (eds.), *Embodying Wisdom: Art, Text and Interpretation in the History of Esoteric Buddhism* (Copenhagen: The Seminar for Buddhist Studies, 2001), 173–175.

22. Pal, P., *Art of Nepal: A Catalogue of the Los Angeles County Museum of Art Collection* (Los Angeles County Museum of Art, 1985); von Schroeder, Ulrich, *Indo-Tibetan Bronzes*, 293–368; von Schroeder, Ulrich, *Buddhist Sculptures in Tibet*, 407–529, pls. 132–173; Czaja, Olaf and Proser, Adriana, *Golden Visions of Densatil: A Tibetan Buddhist Monastery* (New York: Asia Society Museum, 2014).

23. 楊鴻蛟、魏文：《師道—遼樓居藏14至17世紀藏傳佛教上師像》（北京：文物出版社，2015年）。Yang, H.-J. and Wei, W., *Shidao—Liaolouju Cang 14 Zhi 17 Shiji Zangchuan Fojiao Shangshi Xiang (Figures of Gurus in Tibetan Buddhism, 14–17 C.E., in the Collection of Liaolouju)* (Beijing: Cultural Relics Publishing House, 2015).

List of illustrations 圖片說明

1 Shakyamuni, Gandhara, 2nd–3rd century, grey schist, H. 153 cm, Zhiguan Museum ZG1100CF039472
釋迦牟尼佛，犍陀羅，2–3世紀，灰片巖，高153厘米，止觀美術館ZG1100CF039472

2 Standing bodhisattva, Gandhara, 2nd century, grey schist, Tokyo National Museum TC-81
菩薩立像，犍陀羅，2世紀，灰片巖，東京國立博物館TC-81

3 Shakyamuni, Gandhara, 1st–2nd century, bronze with traces of gold leaf, H. 16.8 cm, Metropolitan Museum of Art 2003.593.1
釋迦牟尼佛，犍陀羅，1–2世紀，青銅貼金箔，高16.8厘米，大都會藝術博物館2003.593.1

4 Shakyamuni, Gandhara, 2nd century, red sandstone, H. 72 cm, National Museum, New Delhi L.55.25
釋迦牟尼佛，秣菟羅，2世紀，紅砂巖，高72厘米，新德里國立博物館L.55.25

5 Maitreya, Mathura, 2nd century, red sandstone, H. 167.5 cm, National Museum, New Delhi A.40
彌勒菩薩，秣菟羅，2世紀，紅砂巖，高167.5厘米，新德里國立博物館A.40

6 Shakyamuni, Mathura, mid-5th century, red sandstone, H. 220 cm, Government Museum, Mathura 00.A.5
釋迦牟尼佛，秣菟羅，5世紀中葉，紅砂巖，高220厘米，秣菟羅官立博物館00.A.5

7 Shakyamuni, Sarnath, late 5th century, H. 164 cm, yellow sandstone, Archaeological Museum, Sarnath 4924
釋迦牟尼佛，薩爾納特，5世紀晚期，高164厘米，淺黃色砂巖，薩爾納特考古博物館4924

8 Shakyamuni, Maharashtra, 5th century, bronze, H. 56 cm, Nagpur Central Museum
釋迦牟尼佛，馬哈拉施特拉邦，5世紀，青銅，高56厘米，那格浦爾中央博物館

9 Head of Avalokiteshvara, Hadda, 4th–5th century, limestone, Victoria and Albert Museum 1985.31
觀音頭像，哈達，4–5世紀，石膏，維多利亞與亞厘畢博物館1985.31

10 Shakyamuni, Swat, 6th–7th century, brass, H. 12.3 cm, Palace Museum g186796
釋迦牟尼佛，斯瓦特，6–7世紀，黃銅，高12.3厘米，故宮博物院g186796

11 Shakyamuni, Swat, 8th–9th century, brass, H. 12 cm, Zhiguan Museum ZG1036
釋迦牟尼佛，斯瓦特，8–9世紀，黃銅，高12厘米，止觀美術館ZG1036

12 Vairochana, Swat, 9th century, brass, H. 17.8 cm, private collection J2018-049
毗盧佛，斯瓦特，9世紀，黃銅，高17.8厘米，私人收藏J2018-049

13 Dipamkara, Kashmir, 7th–8th century, (Karkota dynasty), brass, H. 26 cm, Palace Museum g201010 3-4
燃燈佛，喀什米爾，7–8世紀（迦爾郭咤時期），黃銅，高26厘米，故宮博物院g201010 3-4

14 Crowned Shakyamuni, Kashmir, 8th–9th century, brass, H. 20 cm, private collection J2018-009
寶冠釋迦牟尼佛，喀什米爾，8–9世紀，黃銅，高20厘米，私人收藏J2018-009

15 Shakyamuni, Gilgit, 8th century, brass with copper and silver inlay, H. 69 cm, Jokhang 4350
釋迦牟尼佛，吉爾吉特，8世紀，黃銅錯紅銅、銀，高69厘米，大昭寺4350

16 Chakrasamvara, Kashmir, 9th–10th century, brass with copper inlay, H. 20.95 cm, Los Angeles County Museum of Art 85.2.4
勝樂金剛，喀什米爾，9–10世紀，黃銅錯紅銅，高20.95厘米，洛彬磯郡立藝術博物館85.2.4

17 Vajrapani, Western Tibet, 11th–12th century, brass alloy with silver and copper inlay, H. 34 cm, private collection J2018-014
金剛手菩薩，藏西，11–12世紀，黃銅合金，錯銀、紅銅，高34厘米，私人收藏J2018-014

18 Manjusri, Western Tibet, 11th century, brass with silver and copper inlay, H. 104 cm, Jokhang 5046
文殊菩薩，藏西，11世紀，黃銅錯銀、紅銅，高104厘米，大昭寺5046

19 Padmapani, Western Tibet, 12th–13th century, brass, H. 40 cm, private collection J2018-035
蓮花手觀音，藏西，12–13世紀，黃銅，高40厘米，私人收藏J2018-035

20 Shakyamuni, Northeastern India, 6th century, brass with missing inlays, H. 52 cm, private collection Z2018-131
釋迦牟尼佛，東北印度，6世紀，黃銅（嵌件從缺），52厘米，私人收藏Z2018-131

21 Shakyamuni, Nalanda, 10th–11th century, black schist, H. 66.7 cm, Metropolitan Museum of Art 20.58.16
釋迦牟尼佛，那爛陀，10–11世紀，黑片巖，高66.7厘米，大都會藝術博物館20.58.16

22 Shakyamuni, Nalanda, 9th–10th century, bronze, H. 23.4 cm, Indian Museum, Kolkata
釋迦牟尼佛，那爛陀，9–10世紀，青銅，高23.4厘米，加爾各答印度博物館

23 Crowned Shakyamuni, Kurkihar, 10th–11th century, brass, H. 40 cm, Zhiguan Museum ZG1010
寶冠釋迦牟尼佛，庫爾基哈爾，10–11世紀，黃銅，高40厘米，止觀美術館ZG1010

24 Crowned Shakyamuni, Bihar, 10th–11th century, bronze with turquoise, crystal and silver inlay, H. 32.1 cm, Metropolitan Museum of Art 1993.311a-b
寶冠釋迦牟尼佛，比哈爾，10–11世紀，青銅嵌松石、水晶、錯銀，高32.1厘米，大都會藝術博物館1993.311a-b

25 Padmapani, Bihar, H. 13 cm, gilt copper, Zhiguan Museum ZG1121
蓮花手觀音，比哈爾，高13厘米，紅銅鎏金，止觀美術館ZG1121

26 Vajrapani, Nepal, 8th–9th century, gilt copper, H. 27.5 cm, Palace Museum g203373 1/2
金剛手菩薩，尼泊爾，8–9世紀，紅銅鎏金，高27.5厘米，故宮博物院g203373 1/2

27 Shakyamuni, Nepal, 10th–11th century, gilt copper, H. 81 cm, Zhiguan Museum ZG1019
釋迦牟尼佛，尼泊爾，10–11世紀，紅銅鎏金，高81厘米，止觀美術館ZG1019

CATALOGUE
圖錄

STATUES
造像

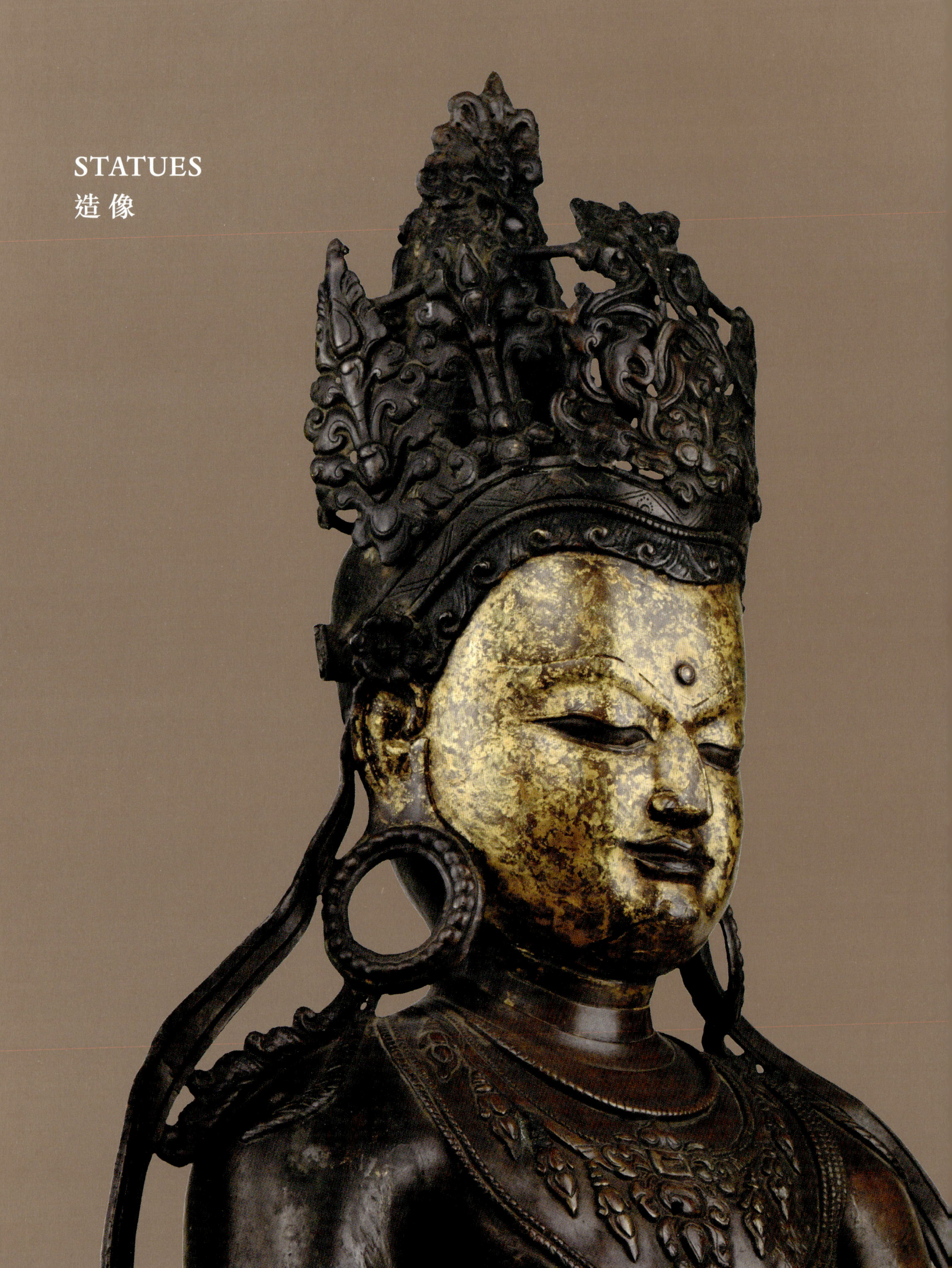

Swat

Located in present-day Pakistan, Swat was previously known as 'Udyana'. Numerous brass statues were produced in this region that incorporate the thick garments for which Gandharan statues are known. This was a popular style in northwestern India and central Asia from the first century. Swat statues also display features of the Gupta school (popular in northern India from the fourth to seventh century), including spiraled hair and V-necked robes arranged in regular folds over taut muscles. Some features of Swat brass statues are also localised: plump faces with wide eyes and flat nostrils and muscular physiques. Ornaments in gold, silver and copper are used on the eyes, lips and *urna*.

斯瓦特

斯瓦特今屬巴基斯坦，古稱「烏仗那」，出產甚多黃銅造像，吸收犍陀羅藝術特色（盛行於公元 1 世紀印度西北至中亞一帶），佛身袈裟厚重，亦承襲笈多藝術風格（盛行於 4 至 7 世紀印度北部），頭梳螺髮，衣領底尖，袈裟貼身，肌肉凸現，衣褶線條排列規整。本地特色則見於其頰頤豐滿，雙目大睜，鼻樑扁平，肌肉剛勁有力，造像眼眸、嘴唇和白毫上錯金、銀及紅銅。

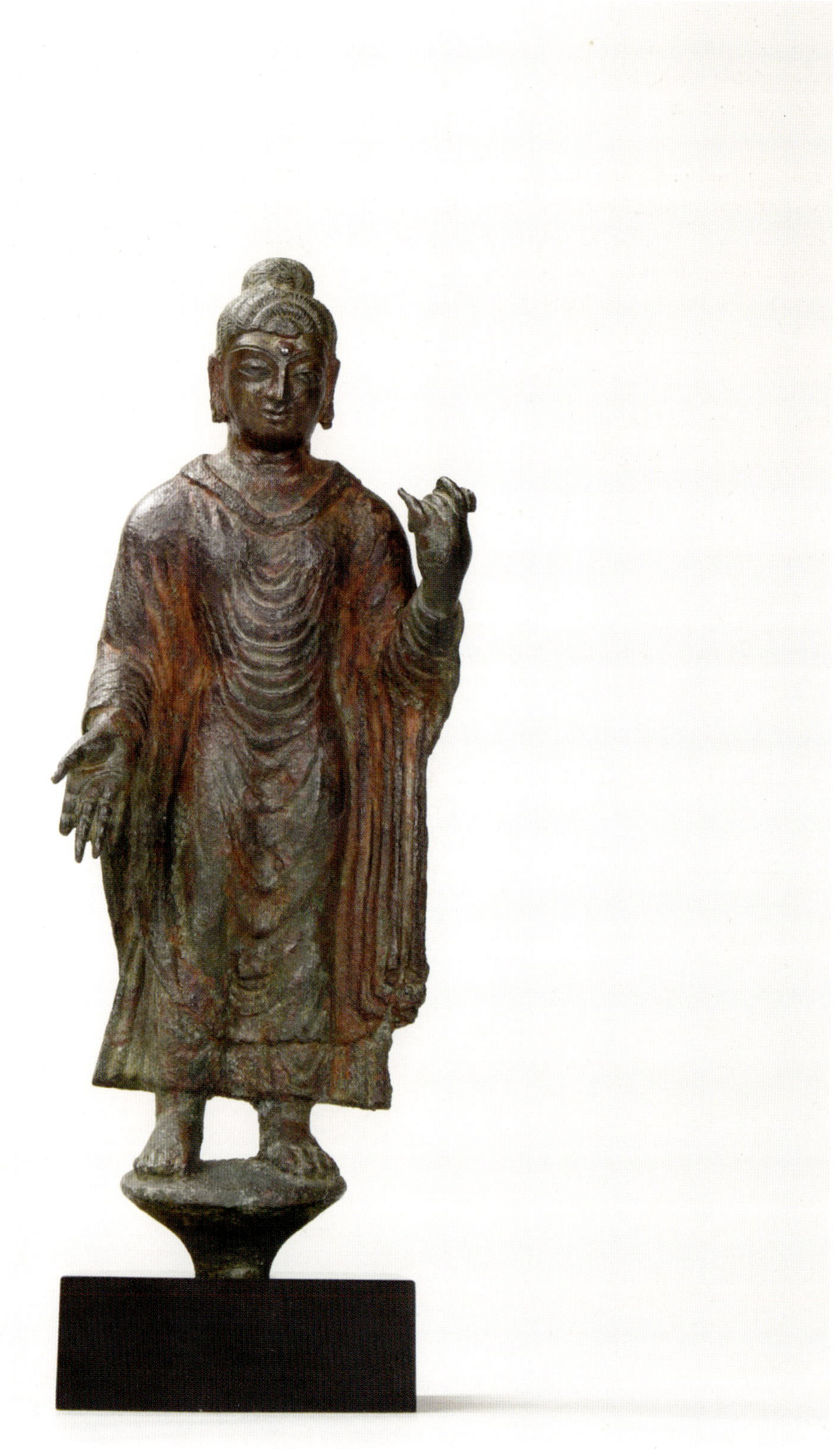

1

Figure of Buddha

Swat Valley, 6th–7th century
Silver inlaid copper alloy, H. 19 cm
Private collection

This figure of a standing Buddha displays some of the features most often associated with the Swat Valley, which incorporated characteristics from Greek sculpture, such as chiselled facial features and hair arranged in fan-like waves. Figures from the region often exhibit the Wish-fulfillment gesture (*Varada mudra*) in the right hand while the left holds the ends of the robe at the left shoulder with proportionally large hands.

Moreover, the style of the Buddha's robe, with a thick hem along the neck that covers both shoulders, is also a Swat Valley convention, as are the heavy pleats along the torso. This robe treatment is clearly rooted in earlier works from the Gandharan region.

佛像

斯瓦特河谷，6至7世紀
紅銅合金錯銀，高19厘米
私人收藏

此佛陀立像輪郭分明，頭髮蜷曲，融會希臘雕塑傳統，屬斯瓦特河谷典型造像。當地佛像多以右手施與願印，左手屈起，執衣角於肩旁，手掌比例略大。衣著承襲犍陀羅傳統，通肩袈裟厚重，領緣較粗。

Literature 參考書目

Rossi, A. M. & Rossi, F., *Symbols of Buddhism: Sculpture and Painting from India and the Himalayas* (London: Rossi & Rossi, 2002), p. 2.

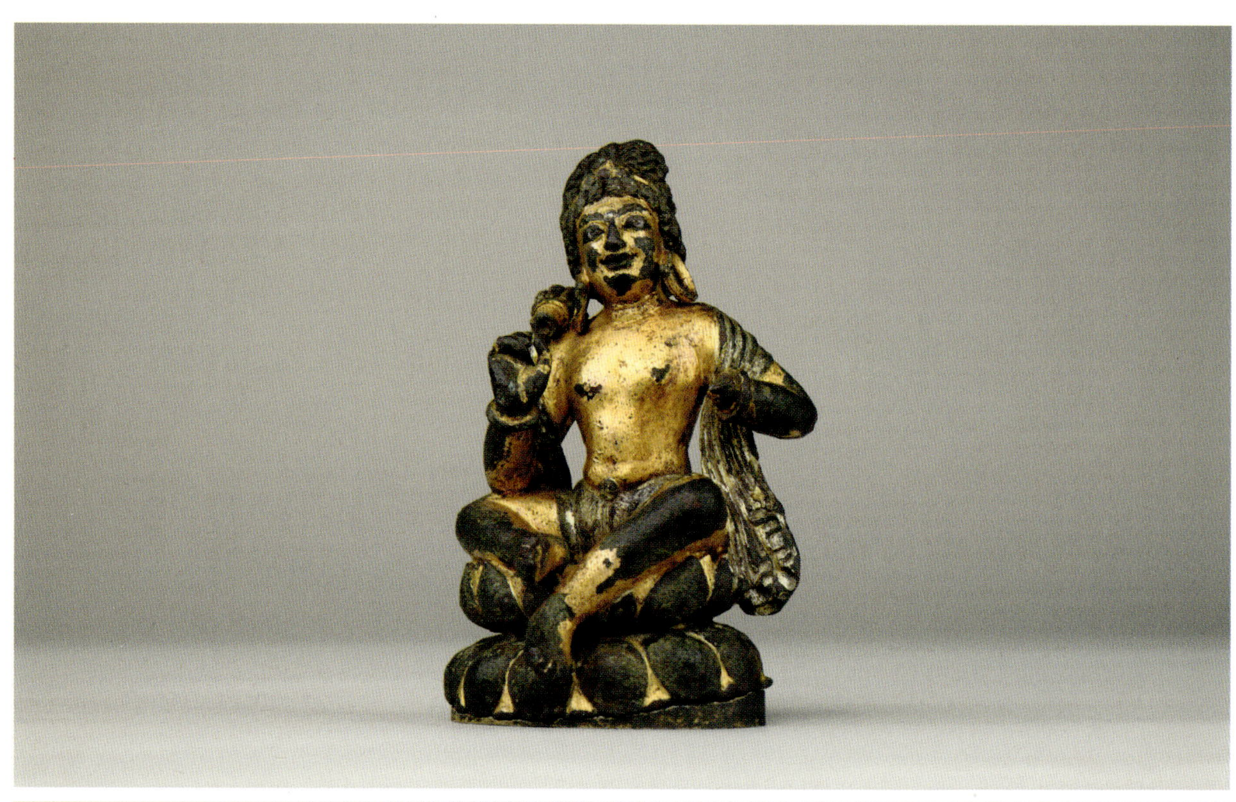

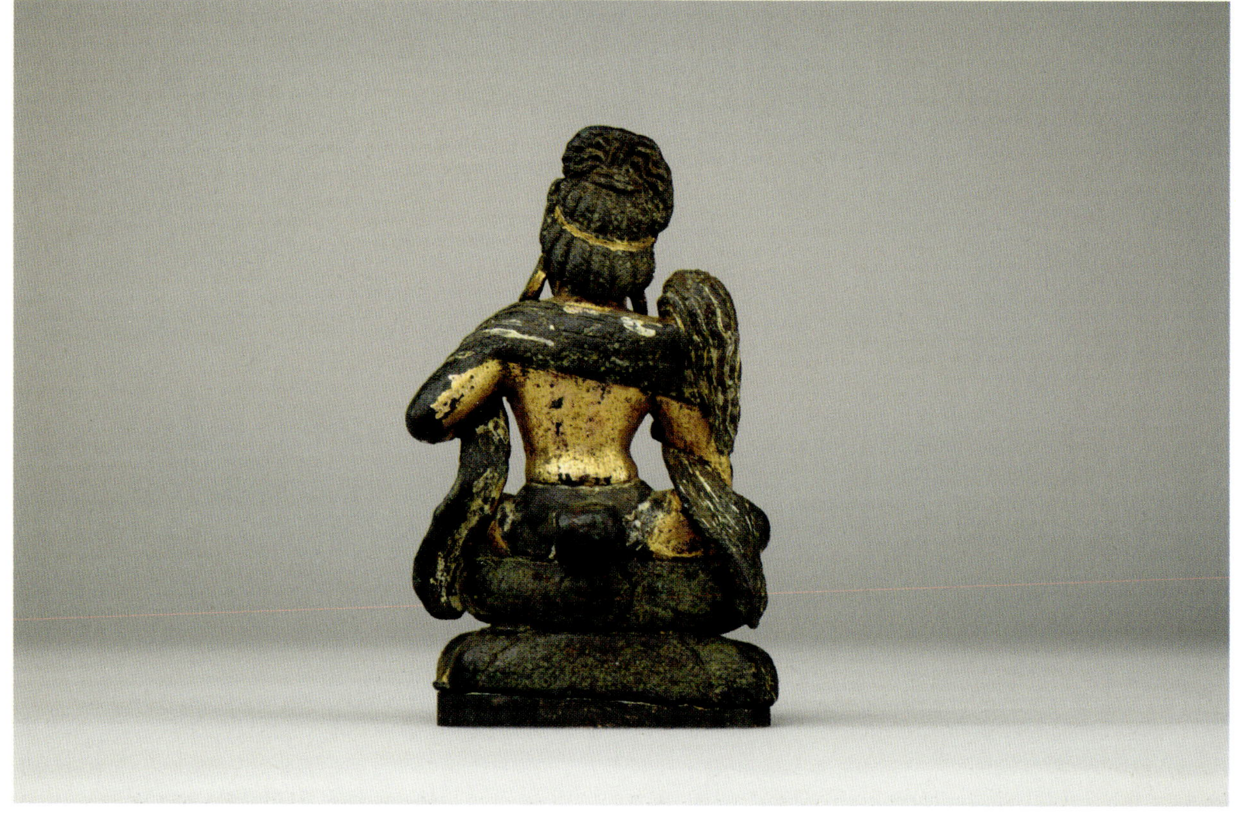

2

Seated gilt bronze figure

Swat Valley, 7th century
Bronze with gold and silver gilding, H. 8 cm
Nyingjei Lam Collection

This unidentified figure has a small diadem secured by a thin gilt ribbon wrapped around the head that makes a slight impression in the hair. Thick locks fall onto the forehead, while longer tresses are pulled upward and secured at the crown of the head, from where they fall in a cascade of thick ringlets. The large tang affixed to the lower torso would have been used to attach the figure to a larger setting.

The excavated sculpture has lost some of its original surface due to corrosion. Still, a large portion of silvering and gilding, techniques mastered in the Swat Valley, remains rich and lustrous, as can be seen on the eyes, flywhisk (its handle now lost), shawl and lower garment. Regional features are also exemplified by the wide, unembellished lotus petals, as well as the fleshy, rounded torsos, limbs and facial features.

鎏金銀青銅坐像

斯瓦特河谷，7世紀
鎏金銀青銅，高8厘米
菩薩道收藏

此像身分尚待辨識。像首戴冠，腰束金帶。曲髮髭至額頭，其餘則紮在冠上，髮端繫以金環。身後設榫頭，供配件接駁。

雖為出土文物，部分表面遭腐蝕，但雙目、拂塵（手柄從缺）、披肩和下身衣著的鎏金、鎏銀仍然濃厚，光澤豐潤。7世紀時，斯瓦特河谷工匠的鎏金銀技藝已相當純熟。另蓮瓣樸素厚重、肢體和面容線條飽滿，也屬當地造像特徵。

Literature 參考書目
Weldon, D. & Singer, J. C., *The Sculptural Heritage of Tibet: Buddhist Art in the Nyingjei Lam Collection* (London: Laurence King, 1999), pl. 1.

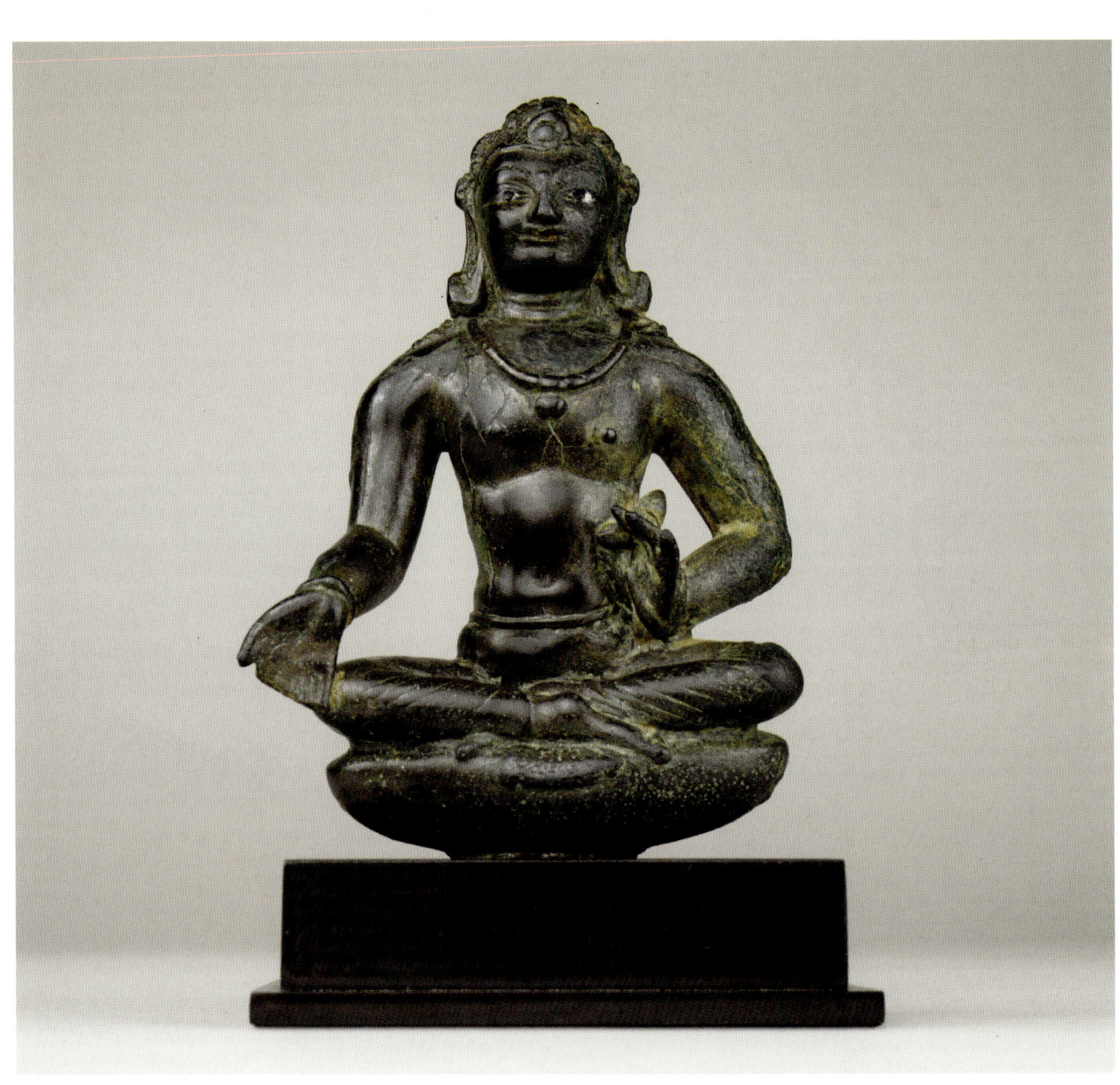

3

Figure of Padmapani

Swat Valley, 8th century
Silver inlaid bronze alloy, H. 14 cm
Private collection

At the hip of Avalokiteshvara Padmapani rests the bud of a lotus flower that has yet to bloom, possibly symbolising his own deferment of nirvana in order to free all living beings from the reincarnation cycle of *samsara*. Though seated in a relaxed manner, his midsection is tightened as if simulating the breath control undertaken by a yoga adept.

He wears a fan-shaped headdress behind his diadem, confirming his attribution to the Swat Valley. Additionally, the simpler treatment of the work's bracelets and necklace reflects an awareness for earlier North-Indian design of the Gupta period.

蓮華手觀音像

斯瓦特河谷，8世紀
青銅錯銀，高14厘米
私人收藏

此像手持蓮花於髖側，含苞待放，象徵觀音之大願——眾生未度盡，不入涅槃。造像腰部收束，展現修行時觀照呼吸的狀態。扇形髮式為斯瓦特造像特點。笈多王朝簡約的設計樣式，也見於造像的項鍊和手鐲。

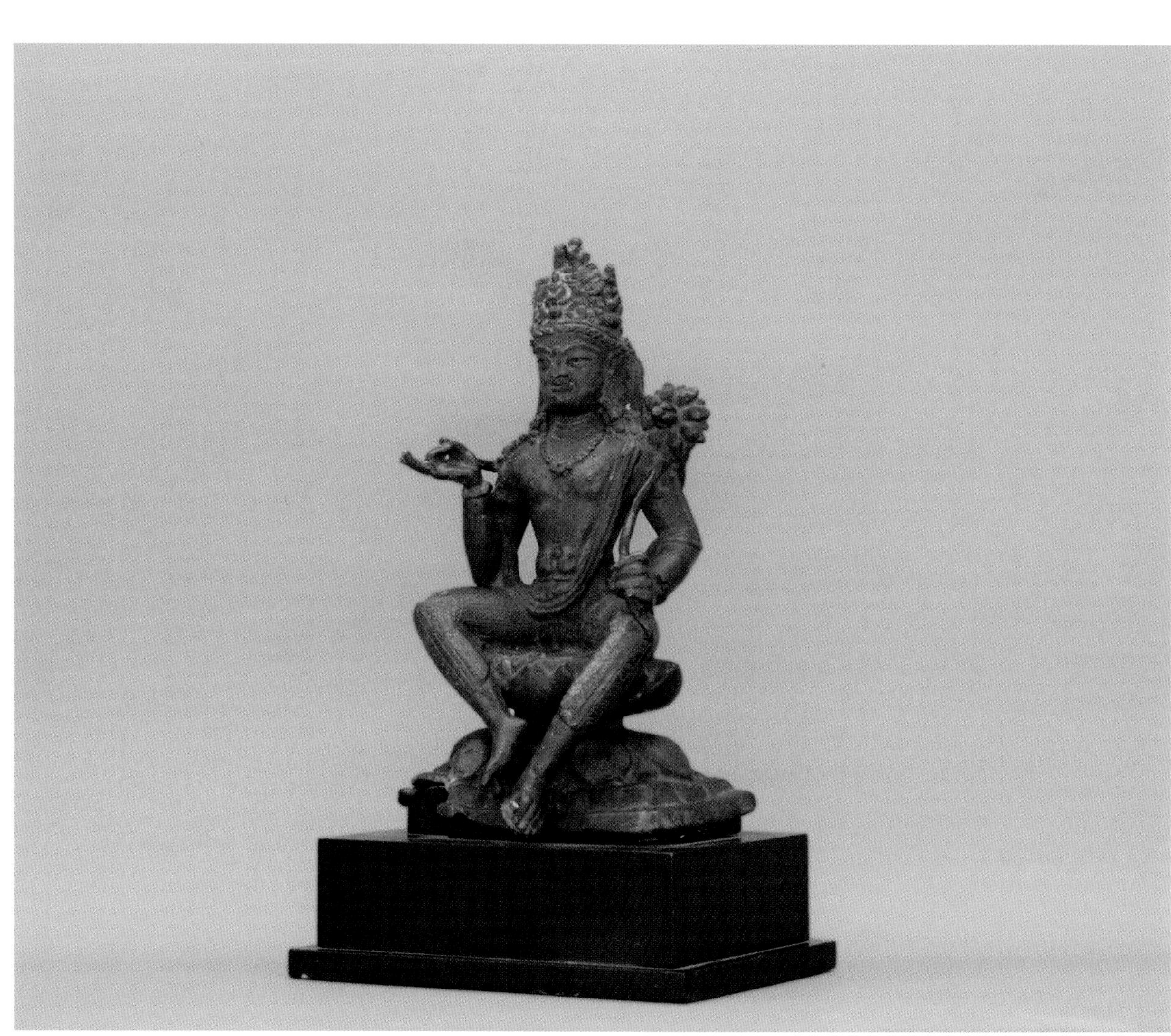

4

Figure of Padmapani

Swat Valley, 8th century
Silver inlaid bronze alloy, H. 14 cm
Private collection

Apart from the lotus flower stem creeping up behind the left shoulder, Avalokiteshvara Padmapani's identity is complemented by a small Buddha Amitabha seated in his crown's centre.

The *Pralambada asana*, also called the European Sitting pose, is common in the Gandharan tradition. Differing from the swollen features and exaggerated proportions of Kashmiri bronzes, the ovular shape of the bodhisattva's head and the narrower treatment of his nose demonstrate the characteristics of figures from the Swat Valley, which are also exhibited by the animated gleam of his silver-inlaid eyes.

蓮華手觀音像

斯瓦特河谷，8世紀
青銅錯銀，高14厘米
私人收藏

此像手持蓮花，蓮莖攀至左肩。菩薩為阿彌陀佛脅侍，故寶冠中央刻有微型佛像。承襲犍陀羅造像特色，雙腳自然垂放，結善跏趺坐，此坐又名「歐式坐姿」，源自西方雕塑傳統。斯瓦特河谷造像頭部多呈橢圓形，鼻型修長，雙目錯銀，更顯有神。

Kashmir

Kashmir is located at the crossroads of India, Pakistan and the Tibetan Plateau. A highly individual artistic style was developed there beginning in the sixth century. Despite incorporating several Gandharan features, Kashmiri art was highly localised: figures are adorned in thin and light robes with well-defined musculature, especially across the chest. Elongated and muscular bodhisattva statues feature floral or pointed crowns. Thrones are designed in the shape of rocks or embellished with animal motifs and ornaments made from copper, silver and precious stones that are applied to seats and garments. Specific body parts such as eyes, nipples and lips are accentuated.

喀什米爾

喀什米爾位於印、巴、青藏高原之交，6 世紀後發展出獨特藝術風格，雖保留部分犍陀羅藝術特徵，但本地風格明顯：佛像袈裟輕薄，肌肉飽滿；晚期菩薩像披長花鬘，戴尖頂或花飾寶冠，身材較修長；坐具設計獨特，如山石座、鳥獸座等；多以紅銅、銀和彩石裝飾坐墊、短裙和身體各部位，包括眼睛、嘴唇及乳頭等。

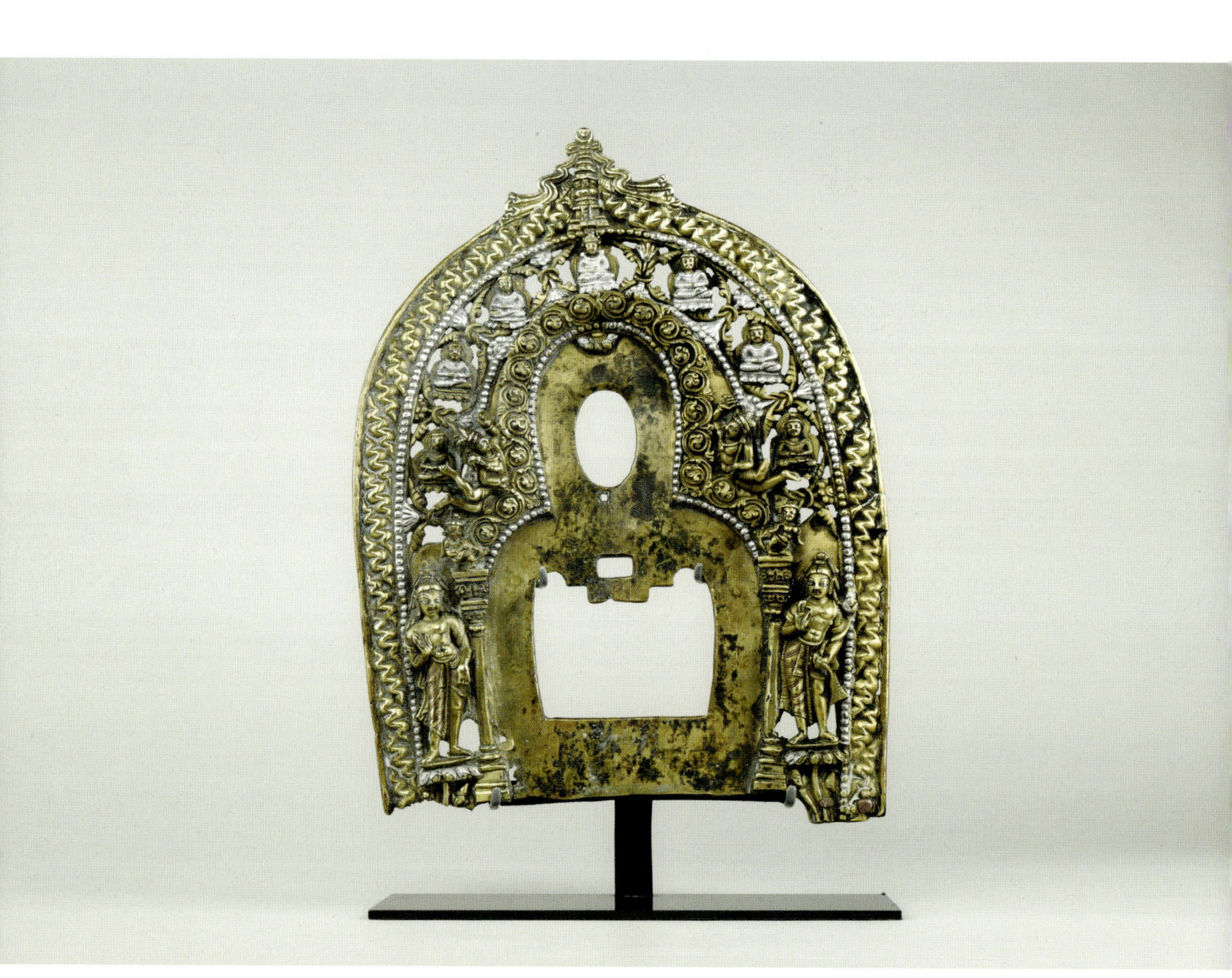

5

Halo for a seated buddha

Kashmir, 8th century
Bronze with silver inlay, H. 29 cm
Private collection

This elliptical halo once provided a backdrop for the throne of a seated Buddha sculpture. Two bodhisattvas flank the space occupied by the central image, standing aside two decorated pillars surmounted by *kinnara*—half-human, half-avian creatures playing musical instruments, behind whose tails are a cascade of scrolls. Seven Buddhas of the Past (assuming the absent figure to be Maitreya, the Future Buddha), or six of them and Maitreya (assuming the absent figure to be Shakyamuni)—are enveloped by interlocking foliage. The robes and eyes of the Buddhas are also highlighted with silver, while copper is used on their lips and in the bodhisattvas' lower garments.

A stupa, a symbol of the enlightened mind, is surmounted by a sun and moon that symbolises wisdom and compassion. Banderoles are attached to the halo's pinnacle. The halo is marked with stylised flames along the outer edge as a gateway of light. The inner boundaries are adorned with silver-laid beads rendered as pearls.

佛像背光

喀什米爾，8世紀
青銅錯銀，高29厘米
私人收藏

此原為一尊佛像身後之背光。兩邊為脅侍菩薩，石柱豎其側，緊那羅立於其上，牽帶花簇。緊那羅為半人半鳥，能歌擅舞，以此敬佛。上方花蔓間為過去七佛（若未來佛彌勒為從缺佛像）；或過去六佛和未來佛（若釋迦牟尼為從缺佛像）。諸佛的袈裟和雙目皆錯銀，菩薩的雙唇及衣裳則錯銅。

背光頂部為佛塔，代表佛的法身，尖頂兩側繫飄帶，上方為日月，象徵智慧與慈悲。內緣滿布仿珍珠的錯銀圓粒，外緣則為火焰，喻示佛身放大光明。

Literature 參考書目
Pal, P., *Bronzes of Kashmir* (Graz: Akademische Druck, 1975), pl. 44.

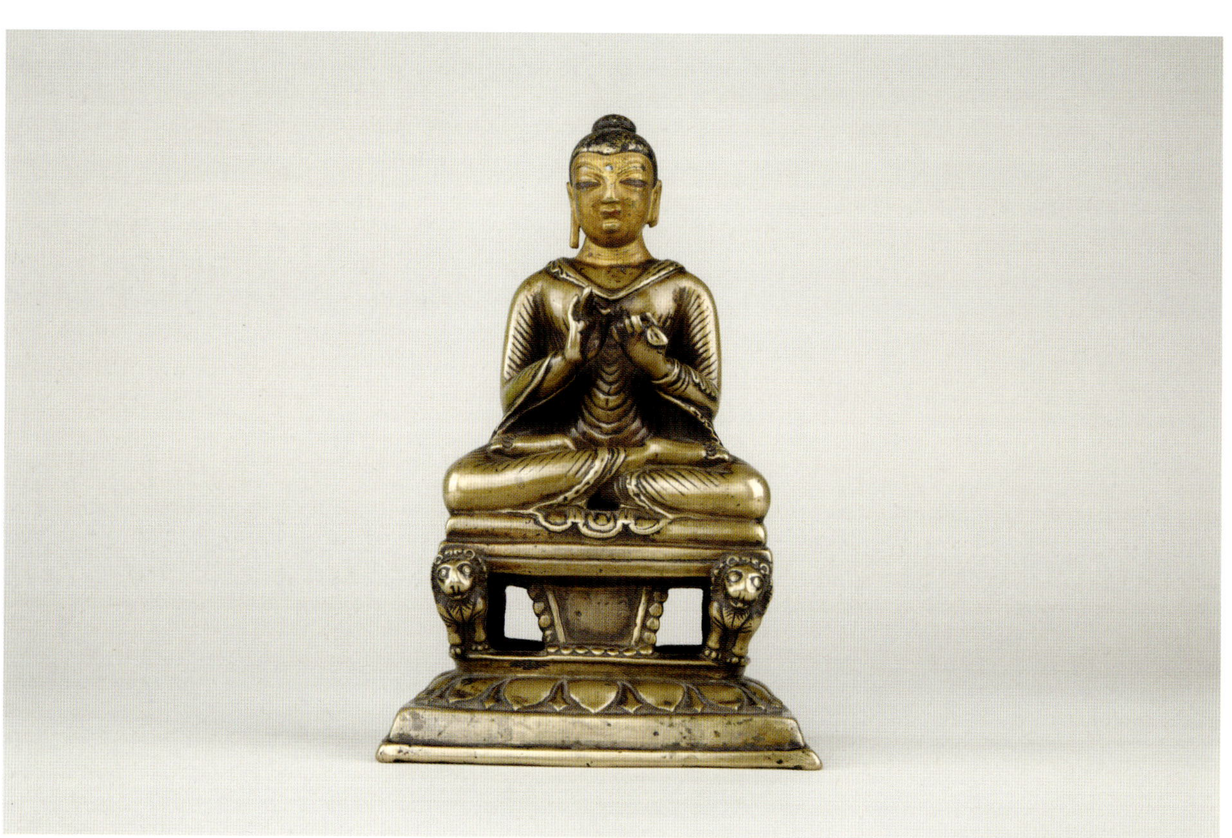

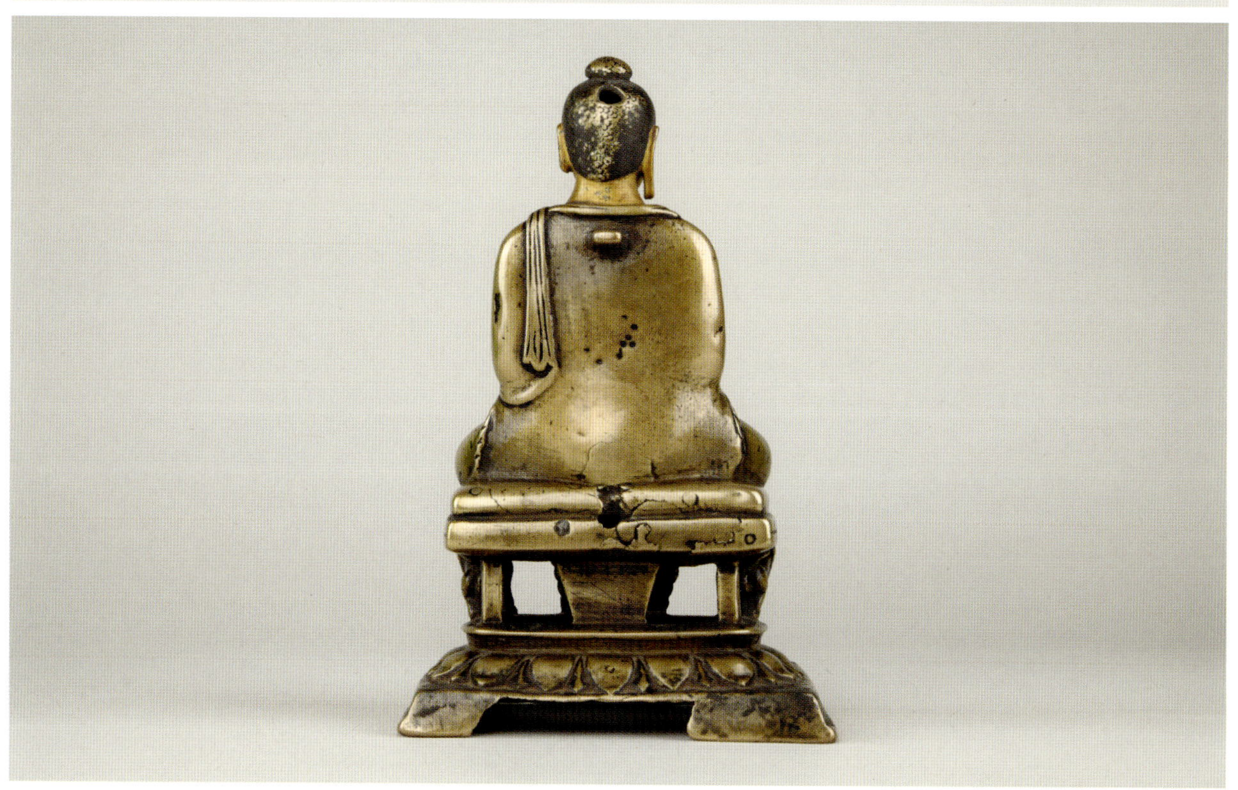

6

Figure of Shakyamuni

Kashmir, 8th century
Copper and silver inlaid brass, H. 24 cm
Cissy and Robert Tang Collection

The figure of Shakyamuni is shown in a re-enactment of his first sermon at Deer Park in Sarnath. His interlocking fingers turn the dharma wheel (*dharma chakra*) as he is seated on a square cushion supported by a pair of lions, which affirms his status. Shakyamuni's shoulders are draped in a diaphanous robe with evenly rippled folds. Behind the figure is a projecting tang along with two holes at the back of the head and cushion, indicating that he once had a separately cast halo.

The robust upper torso beneath the V-shaped collar of Shakyamuni's clinging robe demonstrates the earlier traditions of art from both Gandhara and Gupta that were carried out in Kashmiri bronzes. Other Kashimiri characteristics include the broad nose, distinctive throne designs (animal motifs and downward pointing lotus petals) and silver inlays on the *urna* and almond-shaped eyes.

釋迦牟尼像

喀什米爾，8世紀
黃銅錯銀及紅銅，高24厘米
喜聞過齋藏

此乃釋迦牟尼於鹿野苑初説法時的形象，是為初轉法輪，故雙手結説法印，表示以法輪摧破煩惱，使身心清淨。聖座兩足為獅子形象，以示佛陀尊貴。佛陀身穿通透袈裟，摺痕均勻。背部有榫，頭部、座墊後方均有小洞，顯示此像原有分別鑄造的背光配件。

佛像身材健碩，袈裟現倒三角型衣領，分別為犍陀羅和笈多藝術特色，常見於早期喀什米爾造像。當地造像特徵亦見於其寬闊鼻型、坐具設計獨特（動物造型和蓮瓣下垂）以及白毫和雙目錯銀。

Northeastern India

Areas of Bihar and Bengal in northeastern India came under the rule of the Pala and Sena dynasties from the eighth to twelfth century. Pala statues are distinguished by their bulk, thick and elongated physiques, solemn facial expressions, massive halos, lotus thrones and formalised, elaborately inlaid ornaments. Buddhism was driven out from the Ganges by Muslim troops in the twelfth century.

印度東北

8 至 12 世紀，印度東北的比哈爾和孟加拉地區，受波羅王朝和犀那王朝統治，佛教在印度進入最後的繁榮時期。波羅造像用料厚重、身體寬厚而略長、表情莊重、背光及蓮座高大、鑲嵌裝飾精美。12 世紀，穆斯林軍隊橫掃恒河流域，佛教沒落。

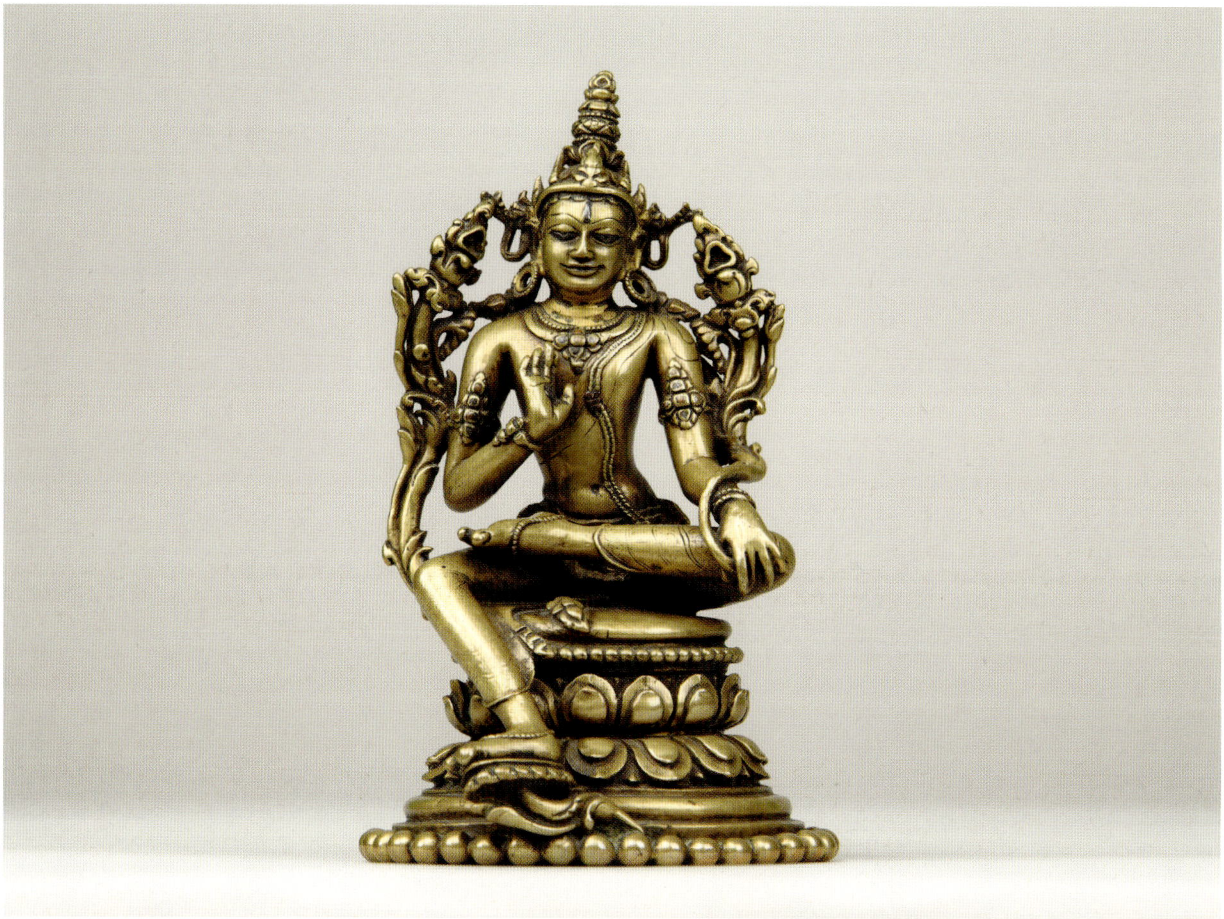

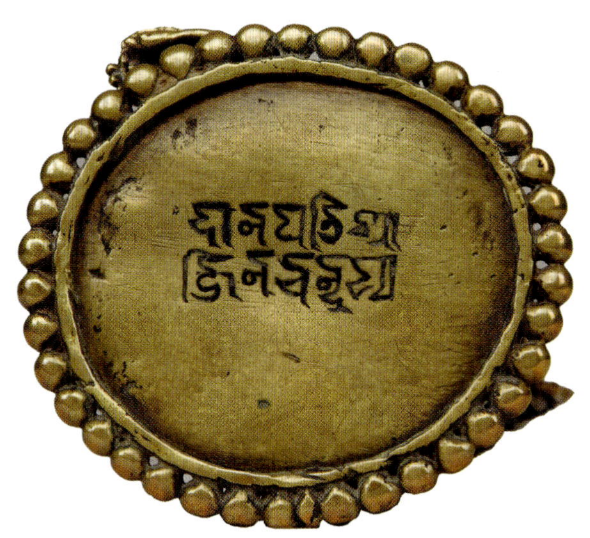

7

Figure of Padmapani

Bihar, Northeastern India, Pala period, 11th–12th century
Copper and silver inlaid brass alloy, H. 14 cm
Cissy and Robert Tang Collection

Padmapani is presented as a princely figure seated in the Royal Ease pose (*Rajalila asana*). Further emphasising his role as a saviour gazing down upon the world, his palm is raised in the Fearlessness gesture (*Abhaya mudra*) as he casts a benevolent expression.

Artistic traditions from the Pala empire can be seen in the elongated eyes, thick lips, tall chignon and elaborate ornaments, in particular the beaded edges along the base. However, the inscribed base plate is not commonly seen among other bronzes from the Pala empire. The traces of cold gilding preserved on the back of the neck suggests that the figure's face was painted with gold in Tibet, where such rituals of empowerment were commonly practiced.

蓮華手觀音像

東北印度比哈爾邦，波羅王朝，11至12世紀
黃銅合金錯銀及紅銅，高14厘米
喜聞過齋藏

蓮花手菩薩坐姿舒坦，為自在坐，施無畏手印，代表觀音之慈悲，具免除恐懼之大威神力，保護眾生修法。

此像眉目深長，嘴唇寬厚，髮髻高聳，裝飾華美，蓮座邊緣飾以聯珠紋，展現典型波羅王朝造像特色，然而底座刻文當時並不常見。而後頸有少量黃金，可推斷面部曾有鎏金，此像或傳至西藏，經開光儀式加持。

Nepal

Beginning in the eleventh century, northeastern India was occupied by Muslim forces. As temples, statues and scriptures were constantly threatened by destruction, many sacred objects were brought to temples in Nepal and Tibet. In this way, Pala objects became models for local artisans. Nepalese statues produced in this period had bulky torsos, a broad and slightly concave forehead, elongated earlobes and thin garments. Delicately adorned with sophisticated motifs, crowns, earrings, jewelled chains and belts were all inlaid with various precious stones and silver.

尼泊爾

11 世紀以降，印度東北被穆斯林勢力侵佔，寺院、造像、典籍被毀，大批僧人逃往加德滿都河谷避難，無數法器流入尼泊爾和西藏的寺廟，為當地藝匠提供豐富的素材，波羅藝術因此成為模仿對象。尼泊爾造像體型豐潤，額寬而略向下凹，大耳垂肩，衣質輕薄，裝飾極盡華麗，尤其寶冠、耳環、瓔珞、腰帶等部分裝飾紋樣繁巧，鑲嵌大量寶石，錯銀甚多。

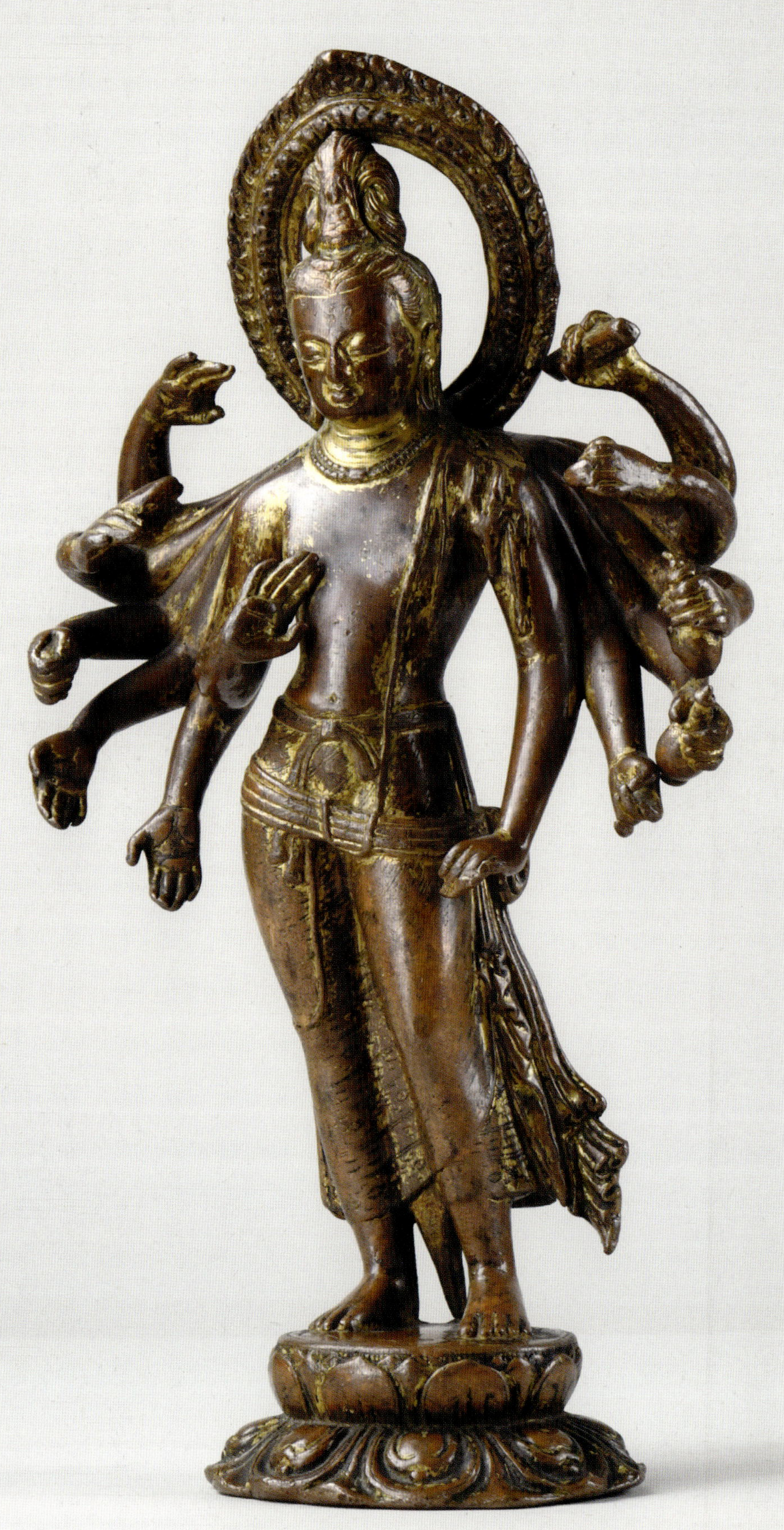

8

Figure of Amoghapasha

Nepal, 8th–9th century
Copper with traces of gilding and pigment, H. 32 cm
Private collection

Amoghapasha is shown here in the *Tribhanga* pose. Dressed simply, the figure includes the sacred thread (*upavita*), antelope skin and a scarf. Amoghapasha's twelve arms are arranged in a fan shape. Unfortunately, the arms have been damaged over the years and are now nearly all displaced.

Amoghapasha is particularly popular in Nepal and rarely encountered in Tibet. However, this image was likely worshipped in Tibet for a significant period of time, as confirmed by the traces of gold paint on the face and neck and the blue pigment in the hair.

The webbing between the fingers is one of thirty-two physical characteristics (*lakshanas*) of an enlightened being. Along with the diaphanous robe, the pronounced nose and the protruding lower lip, these sculptural characteristics were derived from the ideals of the great artistic era of the Indian Gupta kings and were rendered throughout the Licchavi period (fourth–ninth century) in Nepal until the start of the Malla period in the thirteenth century.

不空羂索觀音像

尼泊爾，8至9世紀
紅銅，少量鎏金、顏料，高32厘米
私人收藏

此像以三折肢式站立，衣飾簡樸，僅有聖纓、羚羊皮和領巾。六雙手臂如扇形張開，經年累月，破損甚多，故已悉數置換。雖然不空羂索觀音在尼泊爾更為流行，但其面、頸的鎏金以及頭髮上的藍色顏料，顯示此像應曾於西藏受供奉。

此像呈手足指縵網相，即指間相連如蹼，為佛三十二相之一。其衣裝通透，鼻、唇凸出，皆源自笈多王朝的美學傳統，多見於尼泊爾早期造像（離車毗時期，4至9世紀），直至馬拉王朝（13世紀）沒落。

Literature 參考書目

Weldon, D. & Singer, J. C., *The Sculptural Heritage of Tibet: Buddhist Art in the Nyingjei Lam Collection* (London: Laurence King, 1999), pl. 9.

Ricca, F., *Arte Buddhista Tibetana: Dei e Demoni dell' Himalaya* (Turin: Mondadori Electa, 2004), fig. IV.4.

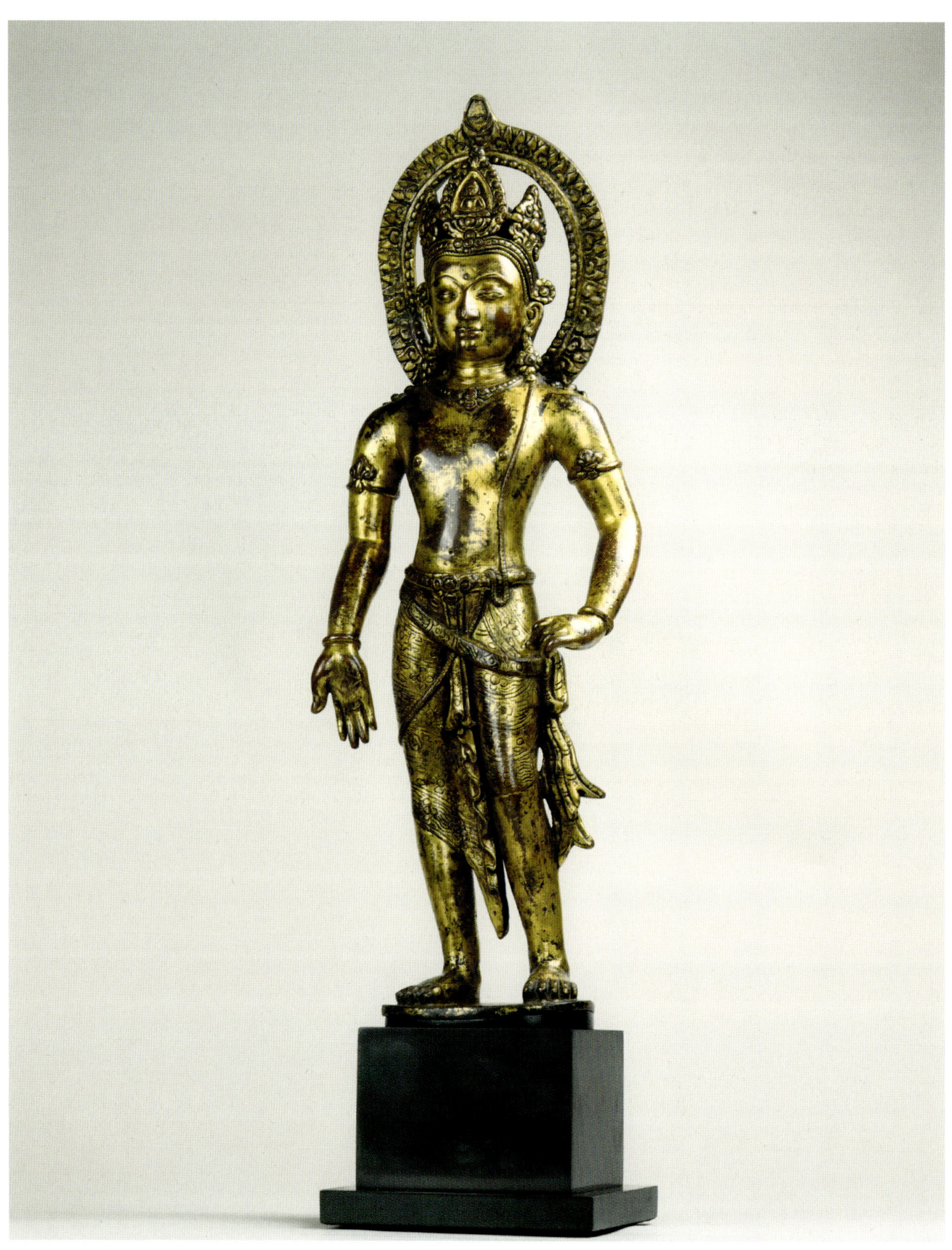

9

Figure of Avalokiteshvara

Nepal, 9th–10th century
Gilt copper alloy, H. 52 cm
Collection of Zhiguan Museum

Avalokiteshvara casts an introspective glance as he lowers his right hand in the Wish-fulfillment gesture (*Varada mudra*). The emergence of the Buddha Amitabha (Padmapani's spiritual ancestor) within the central leaf of his crown solidifies his identity as the Bodhisattva of Compassion.

This poised figure of Avalokiteshvara is a classic rendition of a post-Licchavi period standing bodhisattva. His overall composition, including his heftier proportions, the beaded inner ring of the halo, the asymmetrical length of his lower garment and the crossing of the sacred thread with a diagonal sash at the waist are all features consistent with Nepalese images dating to the ninth and tenth centuries.

觀世音菩薩像

尼泊爾，9至10世紀
鎏金紅銅合金，高52厘米
止觀博物館藏

此像雙目低垂，作冥想狀，右手施與願印。觀世音菩薩為阿彌陀佛脅侍，故寶冠中央有佛像。體型寬厚，背光內緣飾以聯珠紋，裹裙飄揚，聖纓和帔帛繞匝腰間，可見9至10世紀尼泊爾後離車毗時期的造像風格。

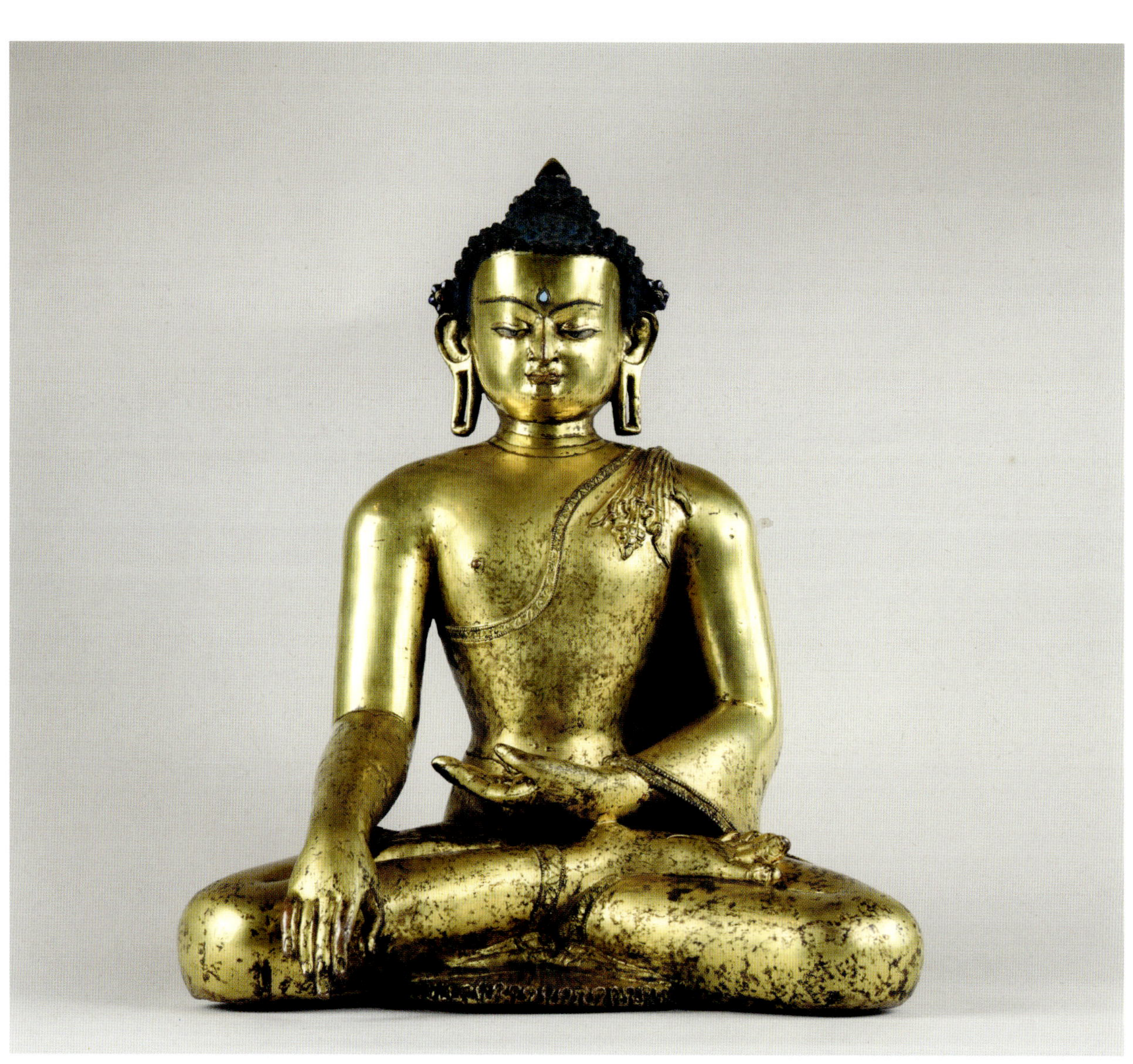

10

Figure of Shakyamuni

Nepal, Kingdom of Khasa Malla, 13th century
Gilt copper alloy, H. 50 cm
Collection of Zhiguan Museum

With his right hand stretched forward in the Earth-touching gesture (*Bhumisparsha mudra*), which symbolises the overcoming of evil forces and obstacles, Shakyamuni encapsulates the moment of his enlightenment and victory over Mara the Demon King in Bodh Gaya in northeastern India. The figure is rendered with downcast eyes, which convey a disconnection from the superficial attachments and concerns of the world.

Shakyamuni's broad torso, wide forehead and nose, thick toes and fingers reflect the Newari traditions of the Kathmandu Valley at the beginning of the early Malla period (thirteenth–fifteenth century). However, the rice-grain pattern on the hems of the robe, the ruby-inlaid flowers tucked behind the ears, and the teardrop-shaped *urna* inlaid with turquoise are attributed to the Khasa Malla kingdom in western Nepal and western Tibet, from where Khasa kings were known to hire artists for the creation of Buddhist images.

釋迦牟尼像

尼泊爾,迦舍末羅王國，13世紀
鎏金紅銅合金，高50厘米
止觀博物館藏

此像右手結觸地印，乃釋迦牟尼在印度東北菩提伽耶證悟時，斥退魔王波旬的印相，故又稱「證成印」，可令一切魔障煩惱悉皆不動。眼簾低垂，表示斷離塵俗掛慮。

釋迦牟尼身軀壯碩、額頭和鼻樑寬闊、手腳趾部粗大，皆反映加德滿都紐瓦爾工匠於早期馬拉王朝時期(13至15世紀)之藝術傳統。而衣緣的聯珠紋、耳背嵌紅寶石花飾、嵌綠松石水滴形白毫，皆為藏西及尼泊爾西部迦舍末羅王朝之造像特色。該國王室曾聘請紐瓦爾工匠，為其製作佛像。

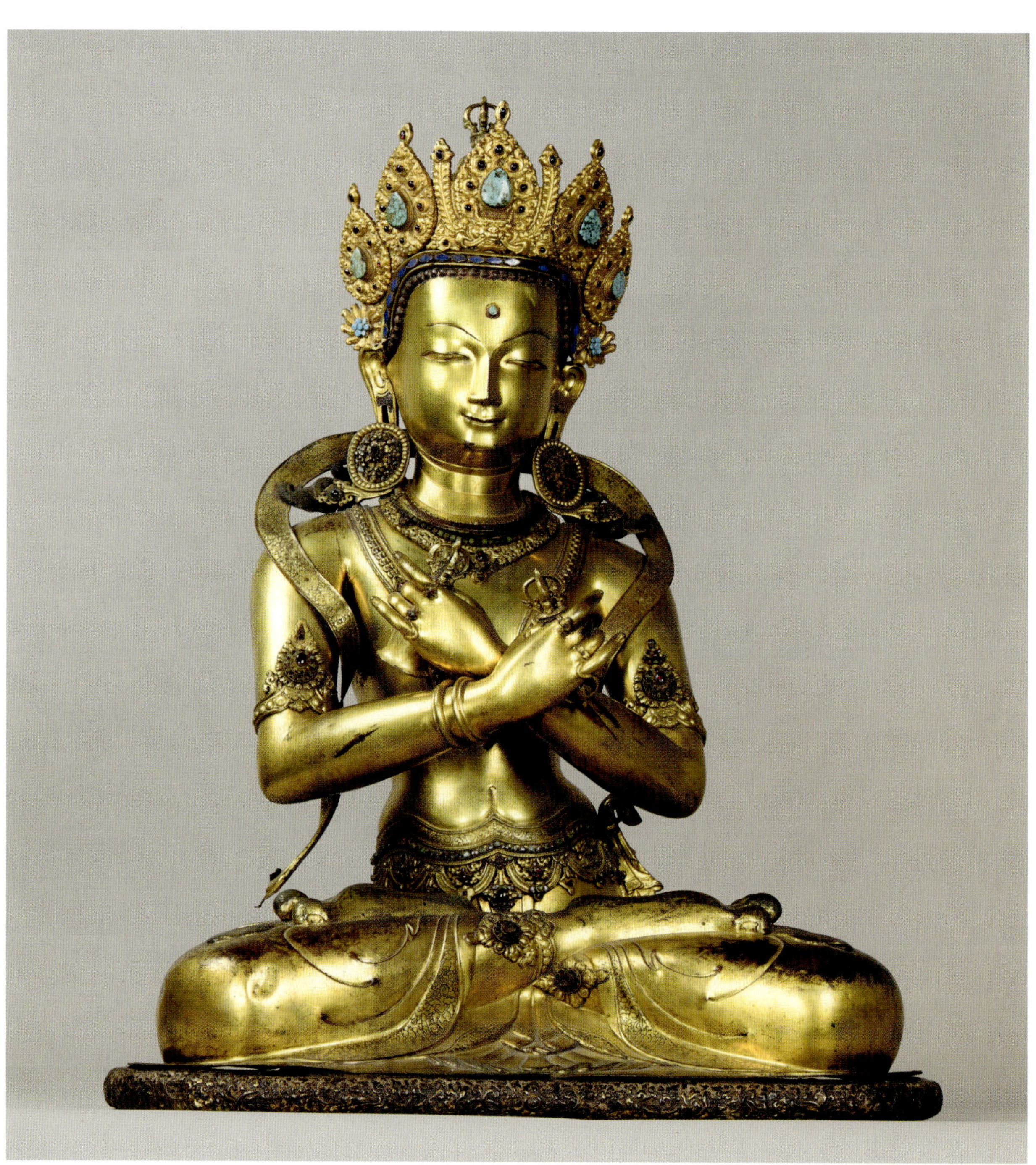

11

Figure of Vajradhara

Nepal / Tibet, 16th century (crown added in the 19th century)
Gilt copper, H. 94 cm
Private collection

The *vajra* and bell held in the figure's hands symbolise compassion and wisdom. Made by Newar artisans, the entire figure is executed in the repoussé technique, except for the hands, which are cast and attached. Only the back of the figure is richly gilded. The stand consists of a thin 'cushion' form of repoussé-clad wood. Vajradhara is well known in Nepal, but his representations are more common in Tibet, so the figure may have been made for a Tibetan patron.

In the repoussé technique, loosely defined as 'hand-embossed', slabs of copper are either hammered, repeatedly turned from front to back in a bed of supporting resin or pitch or, more rarely, pounded out over wooden forms and then riveted and held together by supports. The technique has been a speciality of the Newar artisans of the Kathmandu Valley since the seventh century. The period of the fifteenth and sixteenth centuries was a high point of Nepalese repoussé work, much sought after in Tibetan monasteries as decorations on toranas, stupas, walls and doors.

金剛總持像

尼泊爾/西藏，16世紀(寶冠製於19世紀)
鎏金紅銅，高94厘米
私人收藏

金剛總持像手執金剛杵和金剛鈴，分別代表慈悲與智慧，象徵悲智雙運。此像由紐爾瓦工匠錘揲所製，唯雙手另經鑄造後與像身接駁，除背部外，通體鎏金。其底部木座外緣亦經錘揲加工，作為座墊。金剛總持雖在尼泊爾為人所知，但於藏地更廣為供奉，故此像或由藏人從紐爾瓦工匠訂製。

錘揲鍛造多用於體積較大或作建築裝飾之造像，即將銅片置於樹脂或木製的模上，反覆錘揲成形，各部分再以鉚釘接駁。自7世紀，加德滿都河谷的紐瓦爾工匠已掌握此法，於15至16世紀，更是大為盛行，西藏寺院塔門牌坊、佛塔、牆垣及門上的裝飾，多以錘揲工藝鍛造。

Literature 參考書目

Pal, P., *Nepal: Old Images, New Insight* (Mumbai: Marg Publications, 2005), cover, p. 11.

Central Tibet

Influenced by Pala and later Nepalese art, the Central Tibetan style gradually developed enormous halos, bulky lotus thrones, thick lotus petals, sturdy physiques and sombre expressions. Tibetan artisans also attempted local variations as they produced numerous realistic statues of the founding masters of local Buddhist schools.

西藏中部

沿襲波羅和尼泊爾藝術，西藏中部逐漸形成，造像風格明顯——背光高大、蓮座寬闊、蓮瓣厚重、體格魁梧、表情莊嚴。西藏工匠也製作大量具本地風格的祖師像，甚為寫實。

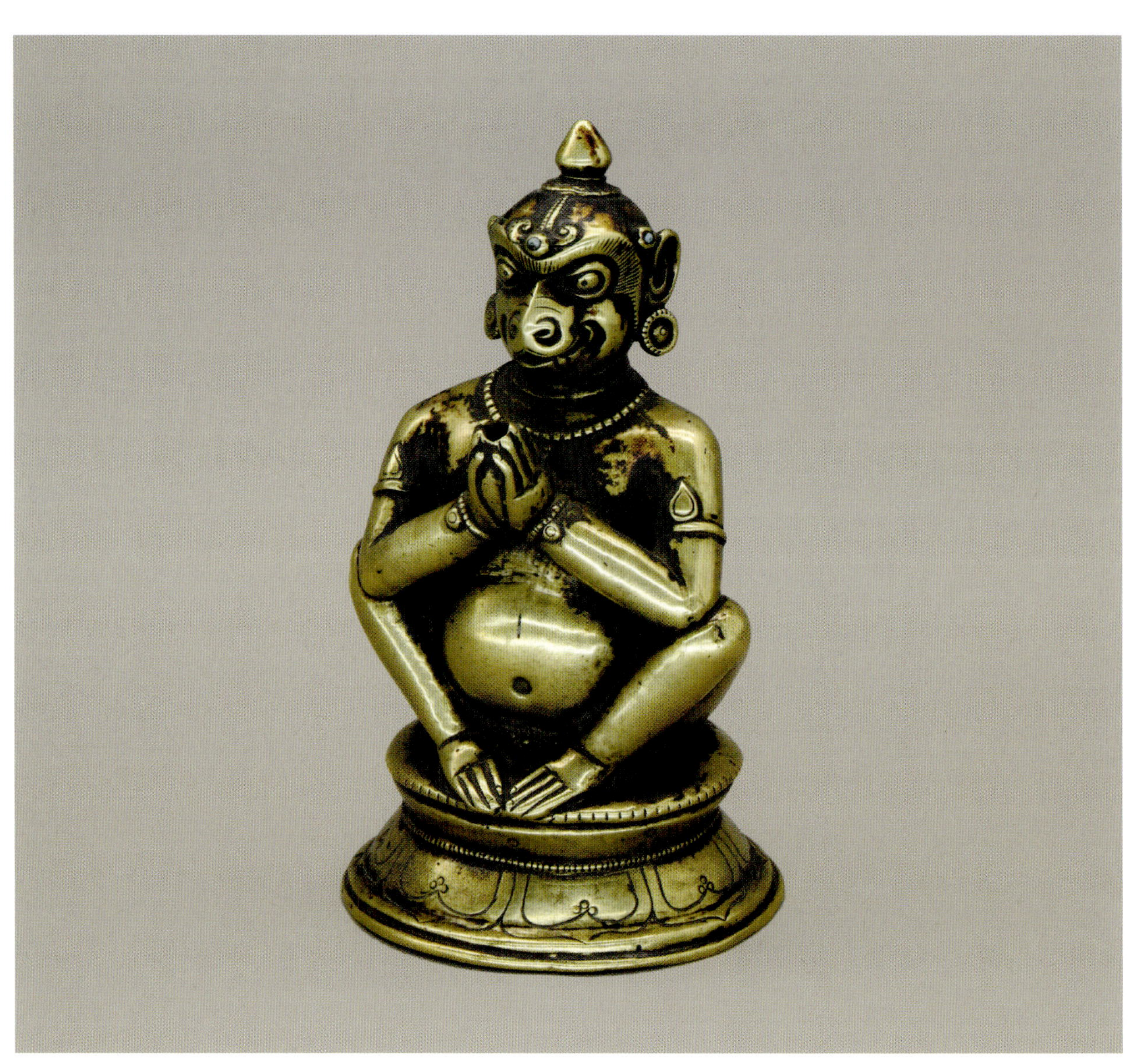

12

Monkey incense holder

Tibet, 16th century
Brass alloy, H. 14 cm
Cissy and Robert Tang Collection

The incense holder is rendered in the form of a monkey with hands in the Offering gesture (*Anjali mudra*). Hunched atop a lotus platform, he exposes his swollen belly, while his neck, ears and arms are adorned with a finial inlaid with turquoise and jewels. Within Tibetan Buddhist art, monkeys typically serve as attendant figures, providing offerings to worldly protectors such as Ganapati, Mahakala and Tsiu Marpo.

猴香座

西藏，16世紀
黃銅合金，高14厘米
喜聞過齋藏

猴香座雙手合十，表示尊崇禮敬，弓背坐於蓮座上，圓腹袒露。頸、耳、腕皆嵌綠松石及珠寶。藏傳佛教藝術中，猴子常隨侍護法，如歡喜天、大黑天和紫瑪等。

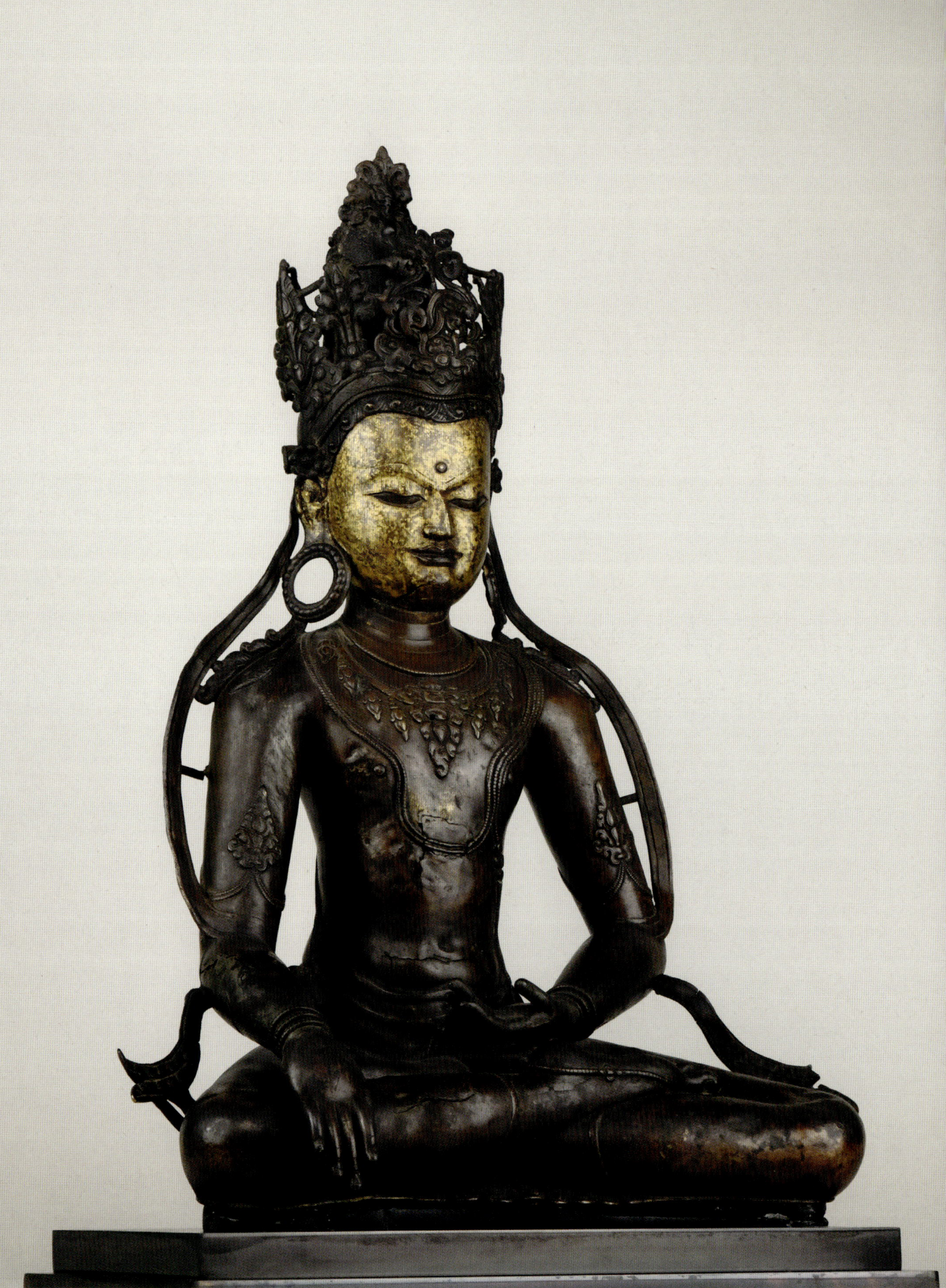

13

Figure of Akshobya

Central Tibet, 13th century
Bronze alloy, H. 58 cm
Private collection

Akshobya is represented in the subtle form of Bliss (*Sambhogakaya*)—distinguished by his outstretched right hand in the Earth-touching gesture (*Bhumisparsha mudra*)—which demonstrates his perseverance over egocentric forces, with his left hand in the Meditation gesture (*Dhyana mudra*).

The late Pala style is seen in the tall chignon and benevolent expression and conveyed through his downcast eyes and upturned lips. The well-proportioned treatment of his face, the patinated surface and the elaborate crown with interwoven tendrils exhibit Tibetan craftsmanship from the thirteenth century.

阿閦佛像

衛藏，13世紀
青銅合金，高58厘米
私人收藏

此為阿閦佛報身像，右手結觸地印，象徵降伏一切魔障，左手結定印，表禪定之意。

髮髻高聳，眼簾下垂，嘴唇微翹，面容慈祥，可見波羅王朝晚期風格。13世紀西藏之造像特色亦見於多處：輪廓比例有致，像身打磨光滑，寶冠精緻，花蔓交錯，工藝精湛。

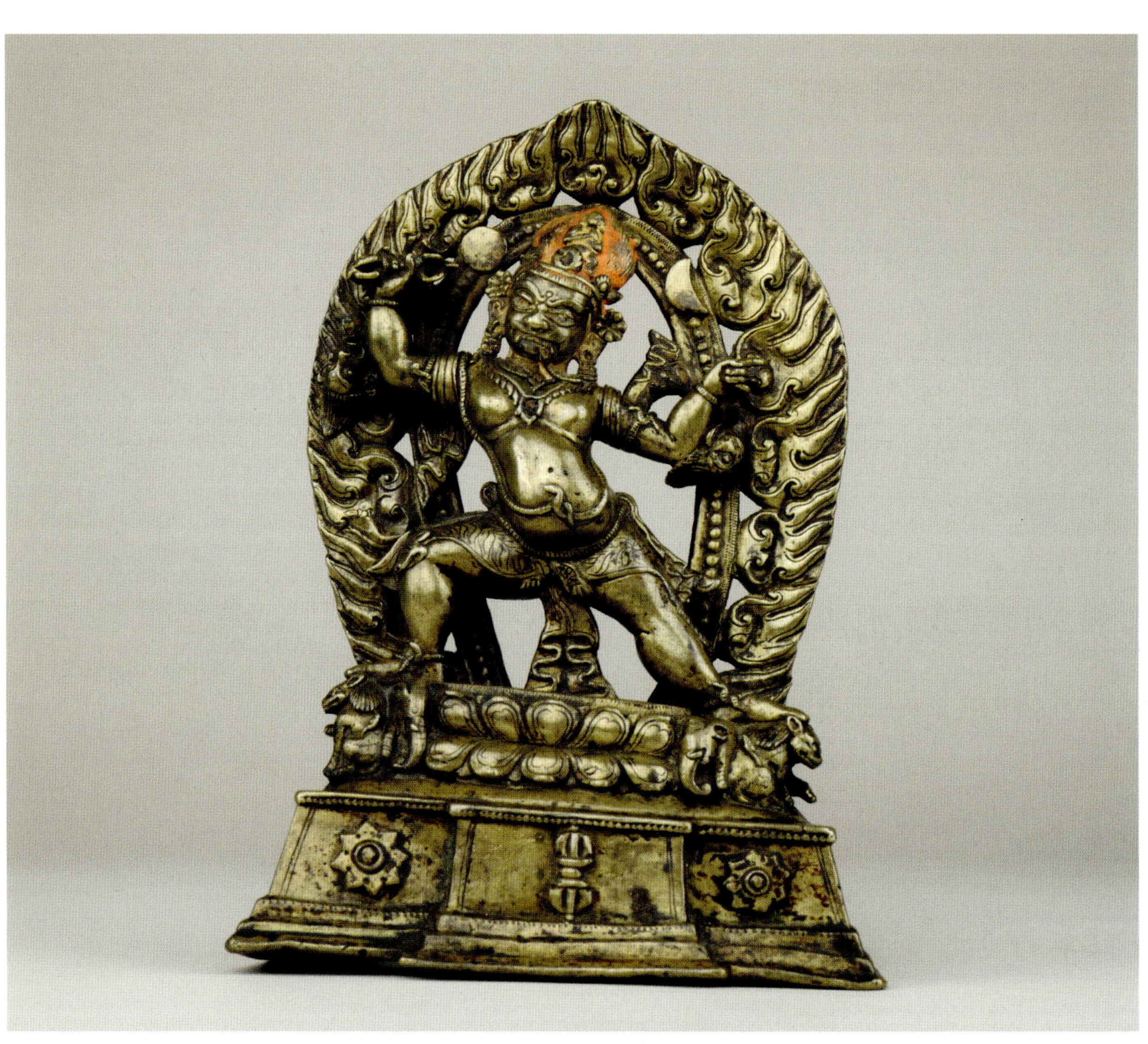

14

Figure of Chanda Vajrapani

Tibet, 12th–13th century
Copper alloy with a white metal inlay and pigment, H. 19 cm
Nyingjei Lam Collection

This wrathful form of Vajrapani assumes the Warning gesture (*Tarjani mudra*), formed by the pointing index fingers on his left hand. His dramatic pose (*pratyalidha*) signifies the hurling of projectile weapons, as he is certainly about to release the *vajra* that is brandished in his top right hand. With elephants and lions underfoot, a tiger skin around his waist and snakes for jewellery, Vajrapani is depicted as a terrifying guardian able to subdue the most dangerous of creatures. This is all the more heightened by his biting a snake and imbibing its poison. Two severed heads representing the devotee's ego are attached to a flaming *prabha* mandala, as are motifs of the sun and moon, symbolising wisdom and compassion.

Stylistically, the influence of the Pala sculptural tradition is evident in the treatment of the sculpture's necklace, sashes and lotus petals. Decorated by an eight-pointed star, symbols representing the dharma wheel (*dharma chakra*), the rectangular throne with a projecting central section, as well as the halo's flames, are also clearly inspired by earlier examples from northeastern India.

威烈金剛手菩薩像

西藏，12至13世紀
紅銅合金、錯白合金、顏料，高19厘米
菩薩道收藏

此尊為金剛手菩薩之忿怒相。造型充滿張力，右腿彎曲、左腿伸展，呈戰鬥姿態。右手持金剛杵，作投擲狀，左手食指豎直，結期剋印，具威脅之意。足踏獅象，腰披虎皮，纏蛇型珠寶，顯示降伏一切猛獸，展現可怖的護法形象。菩薩吞咬毒蛇、飲下毒汁，更顯大威神力。火焰背光兩側各掛日月，代表智慧與慈悲，而倒掛的人頭則象徵斷滅我見。座上的八芒星標誌為法輪象徵。

此像蓮座、胸前、腰間的瓔珞飾物繁多，背光飾火焰紋，底座矩形，中央部分凸出，具印度東北波羅王朝的藝術風格。

Literature 參考書目

Ricca, F., *Arte Buddhista Tibetana: Dei e Demoni dell' Himalaya* (Turin: Mondadori Electa, 2004), fig. IV.25D.

Weldon, D. & Singer, J. C., *The Sculptural Heritage of Tibet: Buddhist Art in the Nyingjei Lam Collection* (London: Laurence King, 1999), pl. 16.

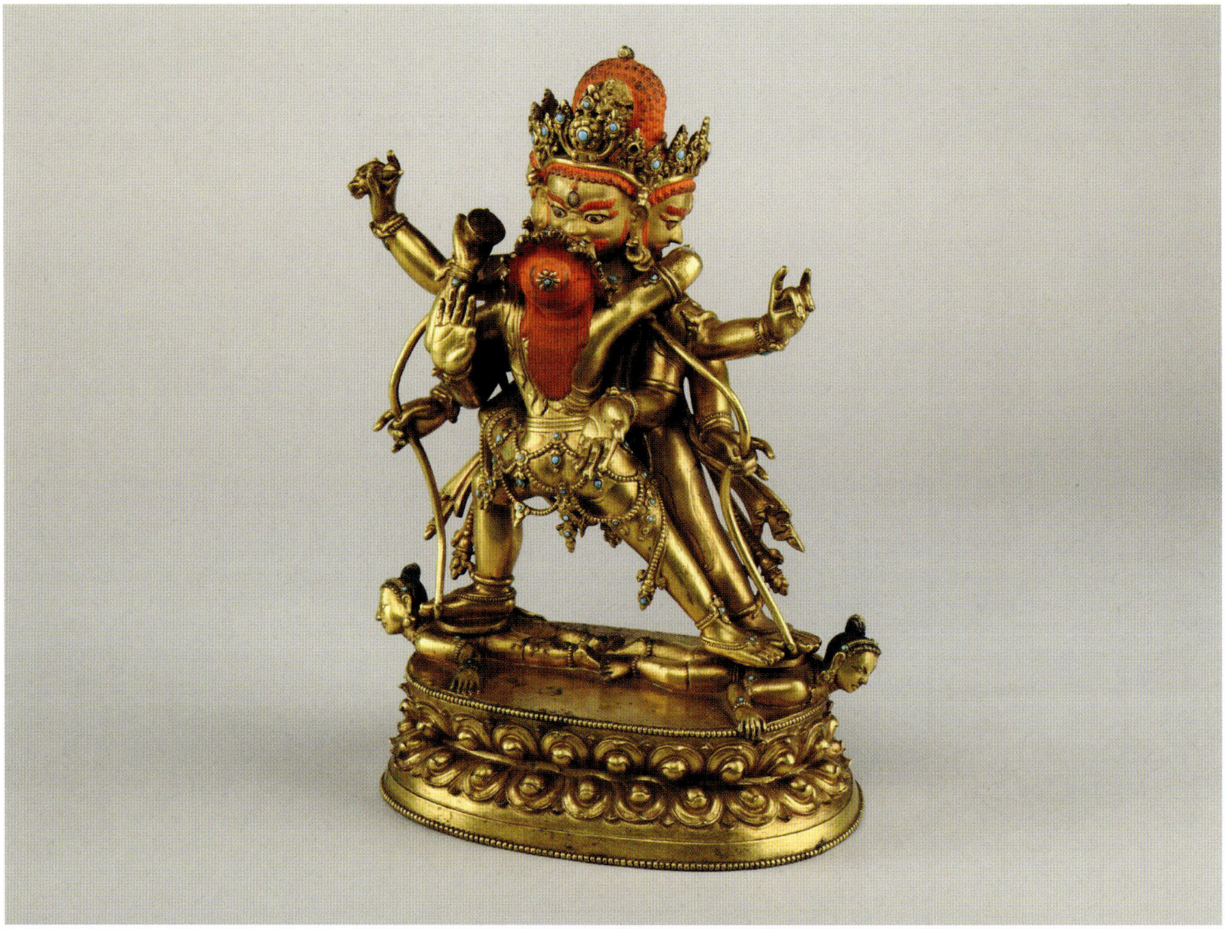

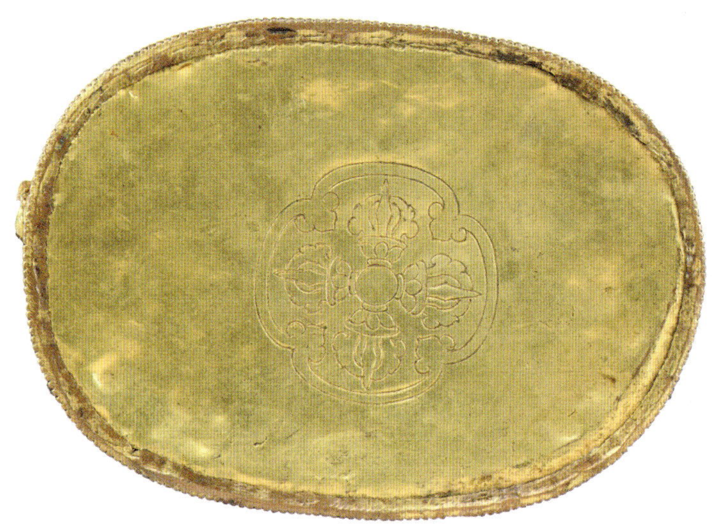

15

Figure of Mahachakra Vajrapani

Tibet, 16th century
Gilt copper alloy, turquoise and polychrome, H. 27 cm
Collection of Zhiguan Museum

The dynamic sculpture of Mahachakra Vajrapani in the tantric position *yab-yum* is distinguished by rich gilding and the vivid use of colour for both the flaming red hair and the intense expressions of the deities' faces. Vajrapani is depicted with three faces and six arms, holding a *vajra* high in his upper right hand, while assuming the Warning gesture (*Tarjani mudra*) in his left hand. He is engaged in sexual union with his consort, who offers a blood-filled skull cup in her left hand and wields a *kartika* in the right. Snakes writhe in and out of his mouth as he tramples on the hostile serpent spirits (*nagas*). Key to Vajrapani's wrathful emanation, snakes or *nagas* convey his role of subduing harmful forces and converting 'poisonous' emotions into virtue.

大輪金剛手菩薩像

西藏，16世紀
鎏金紅銅合金、綠松石、顏料，高27厘米
止觀博物館藏

此為雙身像，即男女雙修的形相。鎏金濃厚，色彩鮮艷，尤見於髮髻。金剛手菩薩三面六臂，右手高舉金剛杵，左手結期剋印。明妃與其合歡，左手持盈血顱器，右手握鉞刀。金剛手菩薩正吞噬纏繞的長蛇(代表龍魔)，腳踏龍魔，象徵降伏魔障，化五毒為正果。

Literature 參考書目
Von Schroeder, U., *Indo-Tibetan Bronzes* (Hong Kong: Visual Dharma Publications, 1981), No. 124 E.

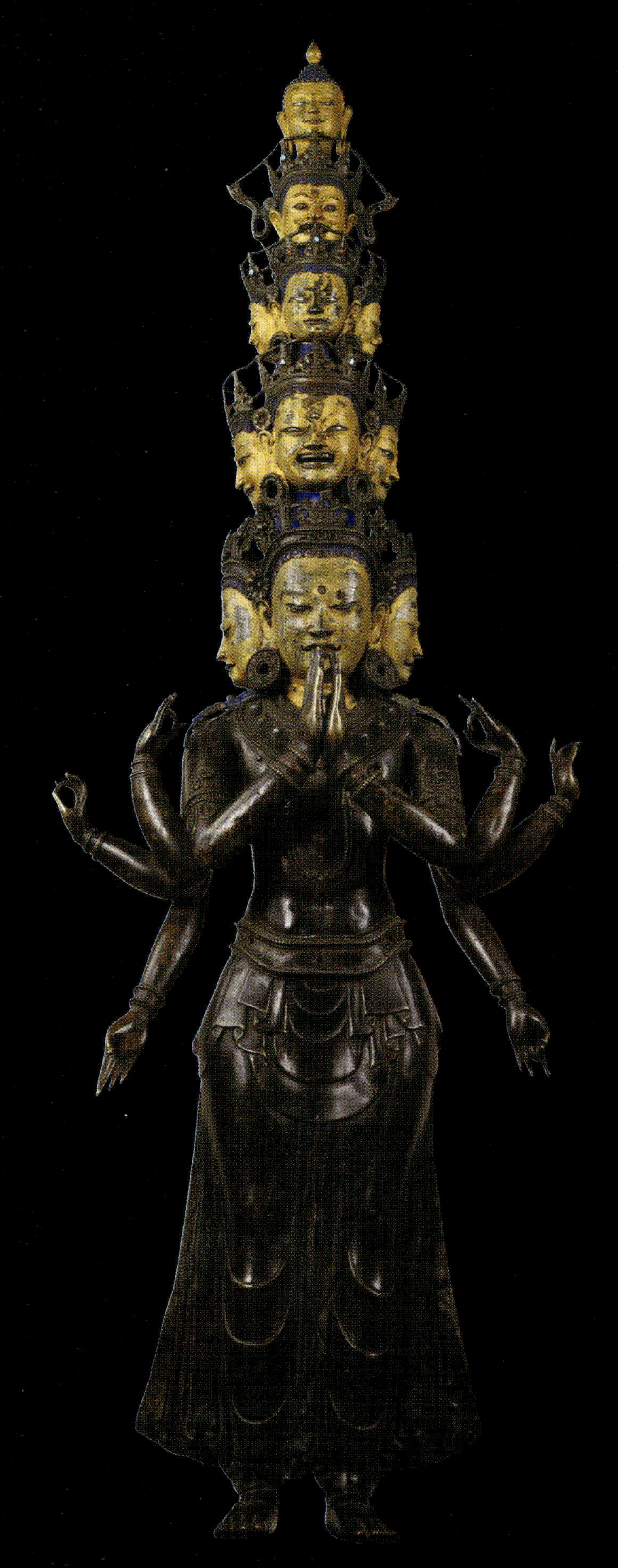

16

Figure of an eleven-headed Avalokiteshvara

Tibet, 14th century
Silver and copper inlaid bronze, H. 121 cm
Private collection

This figure is one of the largest known representations of the cosmic form of the Bodhisattva Avalokiteshvara, with a proportionally constructed tower of heads and fan of arms. The topmost head of the statue represents Buddha Amitabha. The ten heads, with placid, fierce and laughing faces, are all the emanations of Avalokiteshvara when enlightening different beings.

The principal arms are rendering the Offering gesture (*Anjali mudra*), while two others hang down in the Wish-fulfillment gesture (*Varada mudra*) and the remaining in the Fearlessness gesture (*Abhaya mudra*). The circles made with the fingers symbolise the taking of refuge as the union of method and wisdom, and the three extending fingers represent the Three Jewels of the Buddha, dharma (the law), and sangha (the monastic order) as objects of refuge. All of the accompanying objects, which include prayer beads, a book, a bow and arrow, a wheel and a water pot are now missing.

The Tibetan use of silver and copper to enhance the details of non-gilded bronzes is carried over from the Indian Pala period styles imported in the early days of contact. Inlaid silver draws dramatic focus on the whites of the statue's piercing eyes and the teeth on angry faces, while red copper lends realism to the lips and fingernails.

十一面觀音像

西藏，14世紀
青銅錯銀及紅銅，高121厘米
私人收藏

此像最頂一面為如來相，代表阿彌陀佛；為渡眾生，其餘十面，現寂靜、忿怒、笑怒等相。前掌合十，隨後兩手施與願印，其餘結皈依印——兩指結成圓圈，象徵悲智雙運，豎起三指，代表皈依佛、法、僧三寶。原來手持法器，如念珠、書卷、弓箭、法輪、淨瓶等，現已散失。

西藏工匠沿襲印度波羅王朝遺風，以錯銀及紅銅修飾造像的細節，前者用於眼和牙、後者見於嘴唇和指甲，皆使形象更為像真、鮮明。

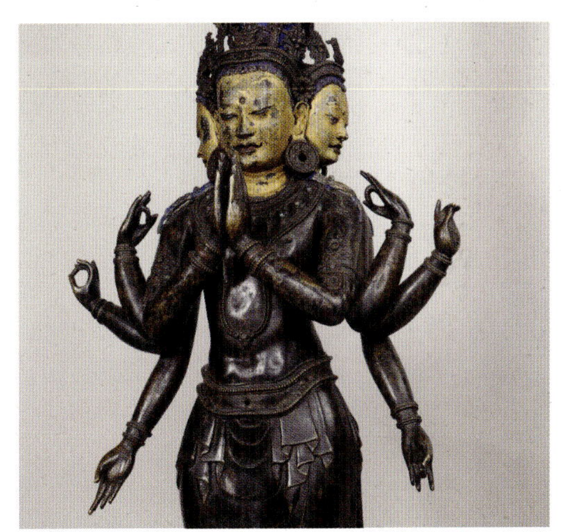

Literature 參考書目
Pal, P., *Himalayas: An Aesthetic Adventure* (Chicago: The Art Institute of Chicago, 2003), cat. 147.
Ekserdjian, D., *Bronze* (London: Royal Academy of Arts, 2012), cat. 77.

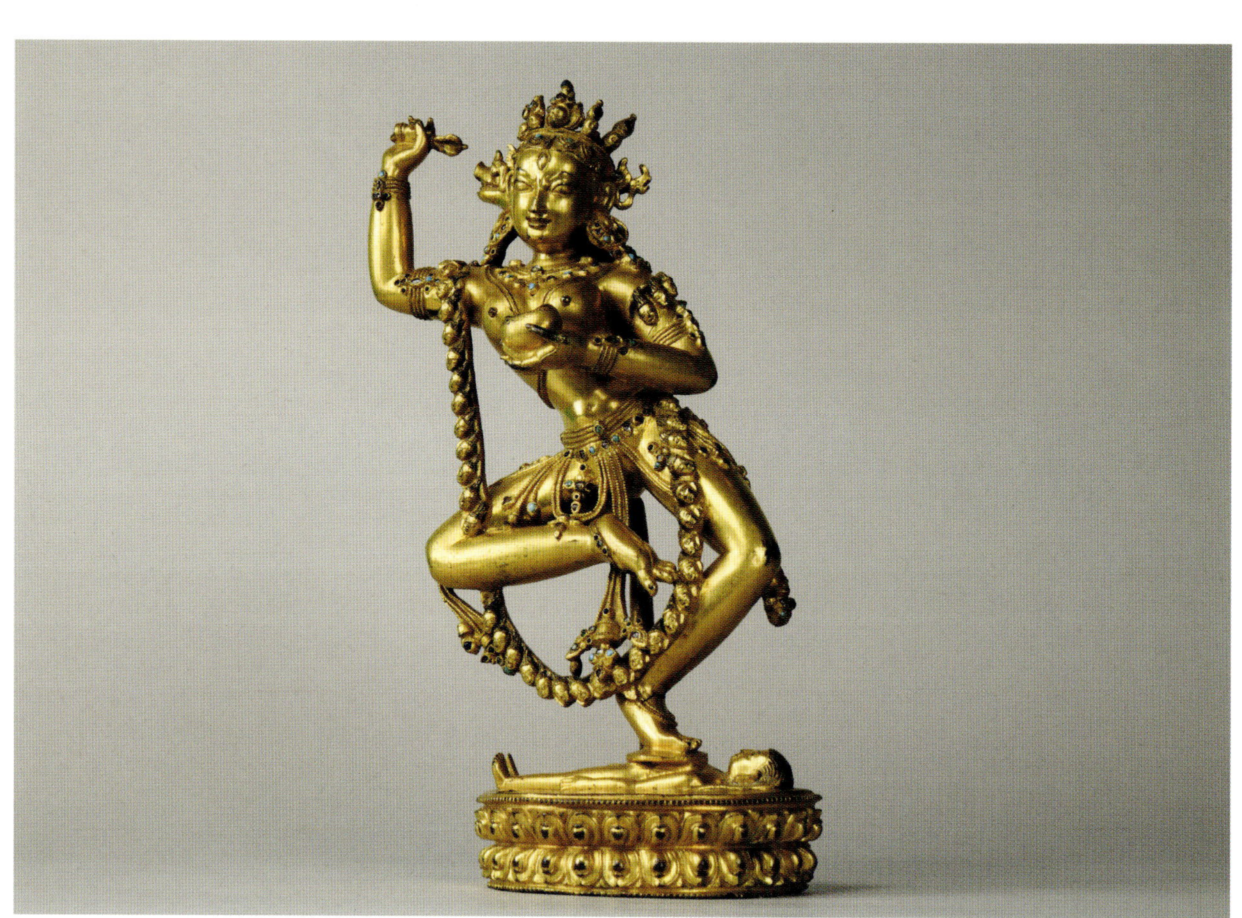

17

Figure of Vajravarahi

Densatil, Central Tibet, 14th century
Gilt copper alloy, H. 36 cm
Cissy and Robert Tang Collection

A wrathful form of Vajrayogini, Vajravarahi is the embodiment of wisdom. She is distinguished by the sow's head protruding from the right side of her face, a reference to her translated name, 'Diamond Sow'. Vajravarahi stands atop a corpse while wearing a crown of skulls and a garland of severed heads, symbolising the impermanence of life. She holds in her left hand a skull cup, a libation bowl for the goddess marking the renunciation of worldly conventions; the curved knife in her right hand serves as a weapon to vanquish demonic enemies. The representation of both items symbolises the union of compassion and wisdom.

The bronze image's powerful limbs, thick gilding, complex use of inlays and the base's densely packed lotus petals exhibit Nepalese craftsmanship under the patronage of the Densatil monastery, the religious stronghold for the Phagmodrupa school, a major branch of the Kagyu order that ruled central Tibet during the fourteenth and fifteenth centuries. The monastery's main assembly hall includes eight multi-tiered, gilded stupas containing countless images known as the Many Doors of Auspiciousness (*Tashi Gomang*). Given Vajravarahi's supreme status, she likely would have occupied the top tier of the *Tashi Gomang*, together with other meditational deities from the highest level of Yoga Tantras.

金剛亥母像

衛藏丹薩替寺，14世紀
鎏金紅銅合金，高36厘米
喜聞過齋藏

金剛亥母是金剛瑜珈母之憤怒相，為一切智慧之母。側面現母豬頭，因豬屬亥，故稱為「亥母」。腳踏屍體，披骷髏冠，戴人頭花環，象徵生命的斷滅、無常。左手持顱器，右手握鉞刀，前者為供養神明的器皿，承載一切福德資糧，後者則象徵斷除魔障之大智慧，兩者兼具是為悲智雙運。

此像由尼泊爾紐瓦爾工匠所製，四肢肌理有致、鎏金濃厚、鑲嵌寶石繁多、底座蓮瓣排列緊密。原供奉於丹薩替寺，屬噶舉派支系帕竹噶舉派。寺內有扎西戈芒佛塔（又稱吉祥之門），由八層鎏金雕塑組合而成。金剛亥母地位崇高，位於佛塔最頂的瑜珈壇城。

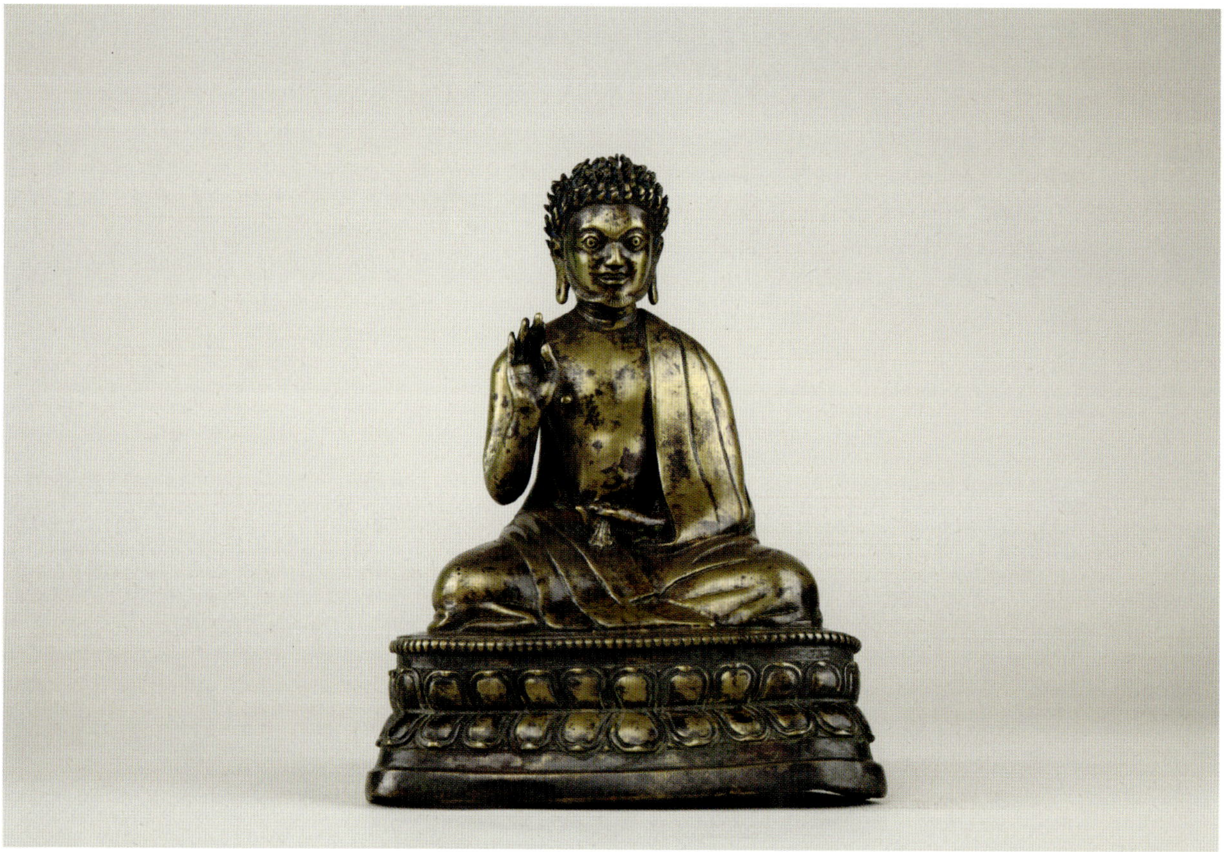

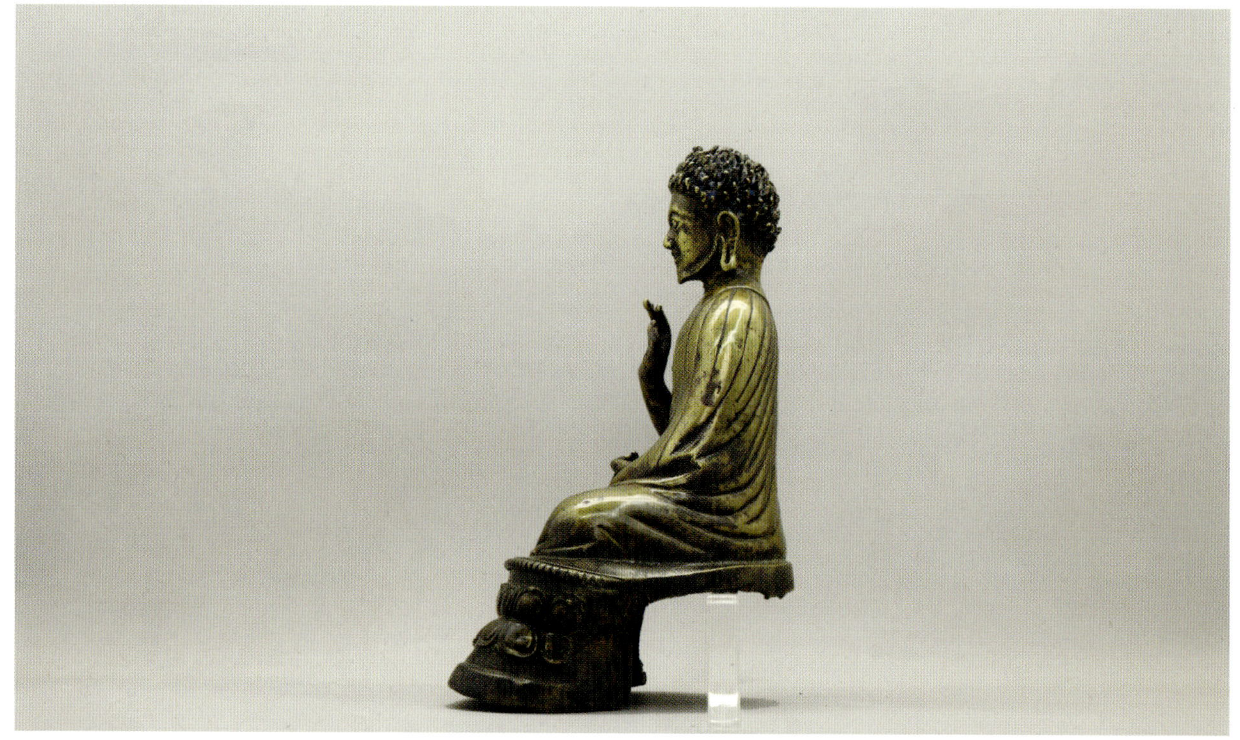

18

Figure of Padampa Sangye

Tibet, 12th–13th century
Copper alloy, H. 25 cm
Nyingjei Lam Collection

The Yogin Padampa Sangye is rendered with wide staring eyes and twisted tresses standing on end. His right hand is raised in the Fearlessness gesture (*Abhaya mudra*) while the left holds the end of his robe. The lotus petal design, with its back containing cut-out shapes, resembles eastern Indian models. A baseplate of iron secures the consecration materials within the figure.

帕丹巴桑結像

西藏，12至13世紀
紅銅合金，高25厘米
菩薩道收藏

帕丹巴桑結為大瑜珈士。瞋目而視，梳螺旋髮式。右手施無畏印，左手執衣緣。承襲東印度造像傳統，蓮座背面經剜空，以鐵板封底，以儲存置於像內的裝藏聖物。

Literature 參考書目

Weldon, D. & Singer, J. C., *The Sculptural Heritage of Tibet: Buddhist Art in the Nyingjei Lam Collection* (London: Laurence King, 1999), pl. 31.

Ricca, F., *Arte Buddhista Tibetana: Dei e Demoni dell' Himalaya* (Turin: Mondadori Electa, 2004), fig. IV.27.

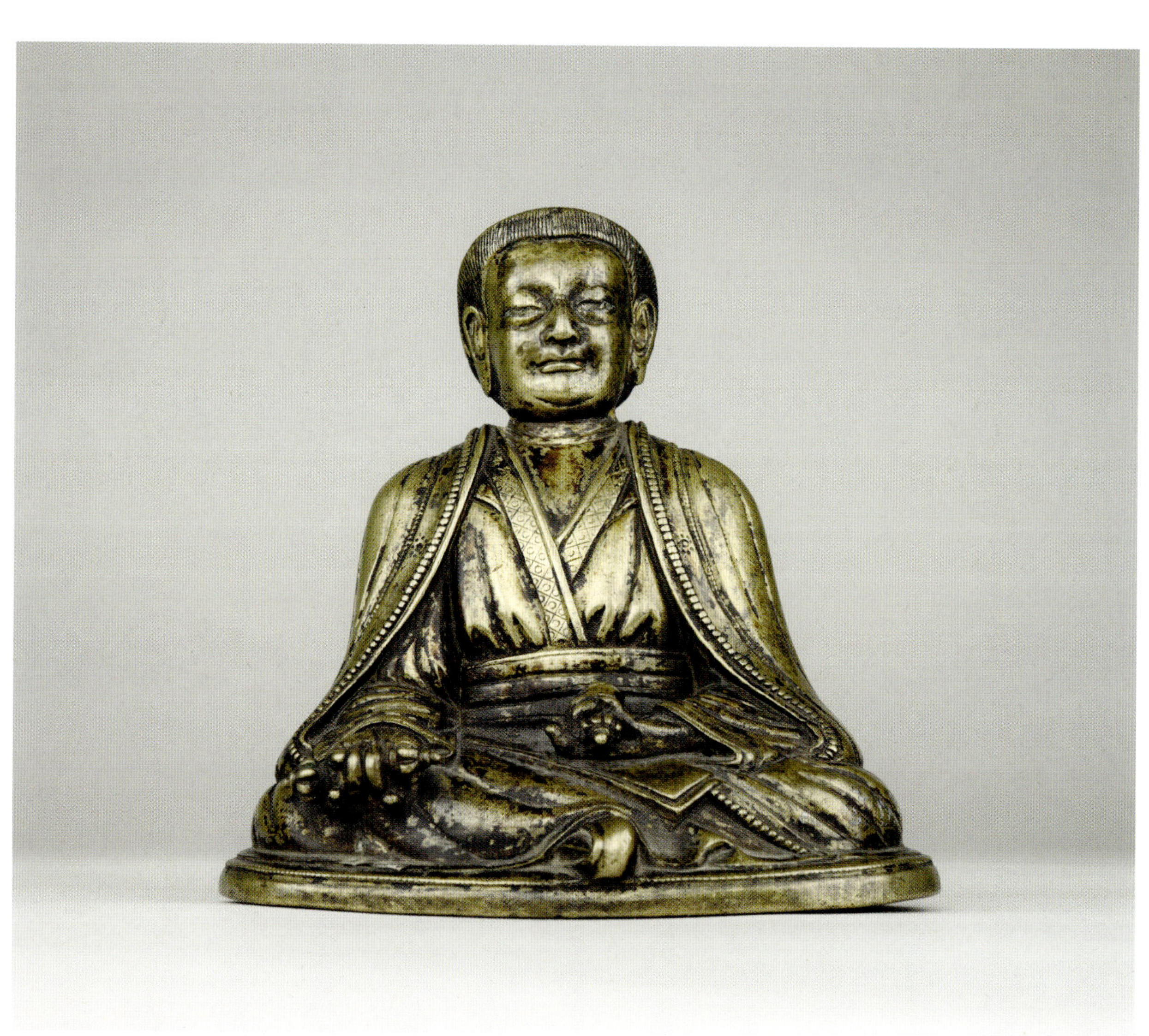

19

Figure of Marpa

Tibet, 13th century
Silver and copper inlaid bronze, H. 13 cm
Nyingjei Lam Collection

Marpa Chokyi Lodro (1012–1097) was a yogin born in southern Tibet who enthusiastically sought Buddhist instruction in India. Marpa was famous in Tibet as a translator of Indian Buddhist texts but he never joined any of the established Buddhist institutions. He was regarded as being the founding guru of the Oral Tradition (*Kagyu*) school in Tibetan Buddhism.

Marpa was a yogin unattached to a monastery. His status as a householder, landowner and businessman is reflected in his clothing, which includes a long-sleeved robe secured at the waist by a thick sash, heavy outer cloak and boots. His long hair is combed into a whorl at the crown of his head. He holds a *vajra* and bell, in accordance with one of his traditional iconographic forms.

瑪爾巴像

西藏，13世紀
青銅錯銀及紅銅，高13厘米
菩薩道收藏

瑪爾巴譯師（1012–1097年），本名卻吉羅珠，生於西藏南部，多次前往印度求法，並將佛典譯作藏文，但他沒有創立宗派或加入寺院，後西藏噶舉傳承奉為上師。

瑪爾巴乃在家修行的瑜伽士，同時是地主和商賈，其身分見於裝束之上：身穿長袍長靴，繫寬腰帶，披厚斗篷，頭髮盤成螺狀。手持金剛杵和金剛鈴的造型，屬傳統圖像樣式。

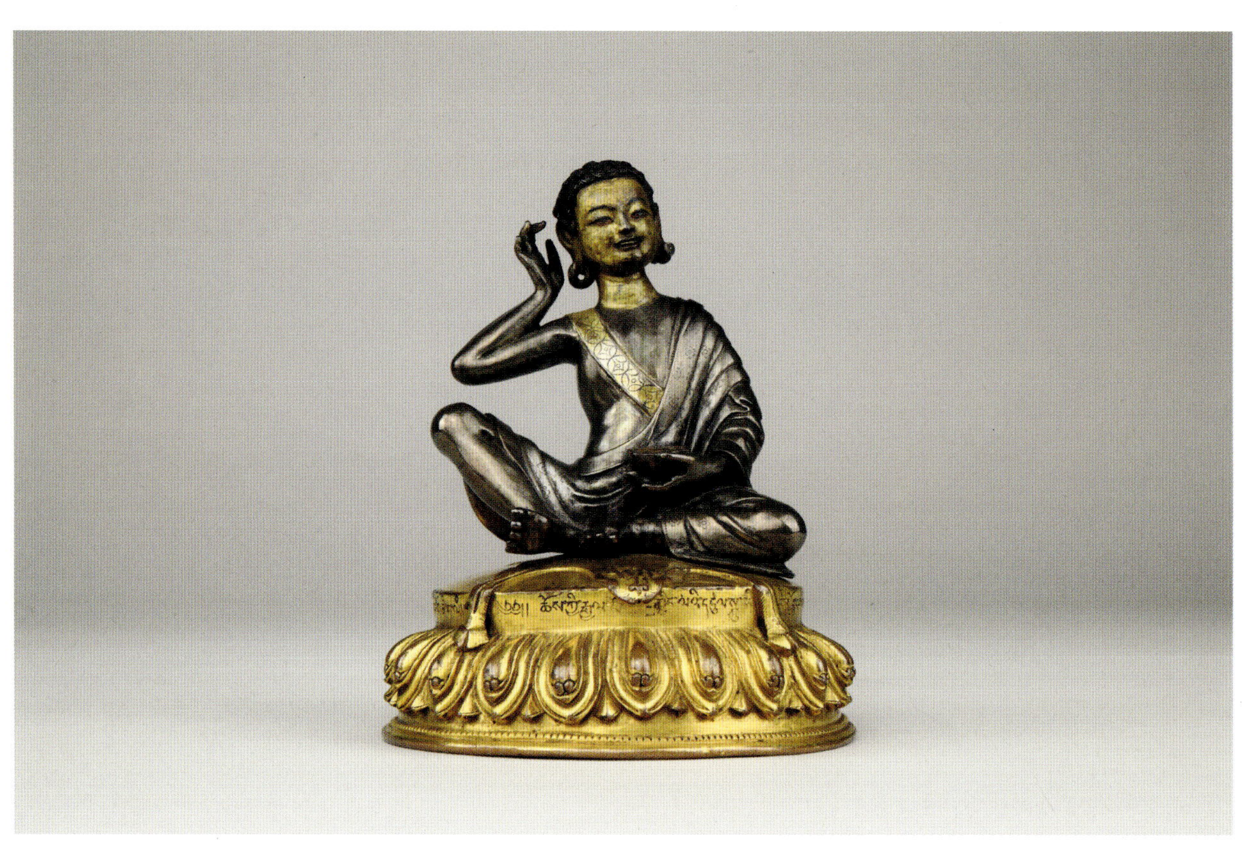

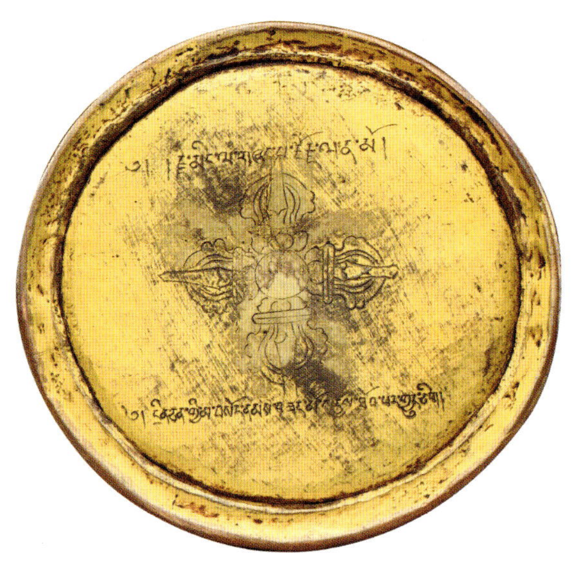

20

Figure of Milarepa
Central Tibet, 15th–16th century
Parcel gilt silver with gilt bronze base, H. 13 cm
Nyingjei Lam Collection

Milarepa (1040–1123), a singing saint and progenitor of the Kagyu lineage, was Marpa's student. He was referred to Marpa by another teacher who was unable to provide effective instruction. Marpa, aware that Milarepa first had to purify himself from the negative karma he had accumulated, exposed him to an extremely demanding apprenticeship. Marpa eventually passed on all of his teachings and Milarepa eventually achieved spiritual liberation. In the figure, Milarepa's parted lips suggest the singing of the songs for which he is famed throughout Tibet.

Inscription (lotus petal base):
This silver image of Mila[repa], king of the sacred doctrine, was set up at Nyug Peak by monk Gagi Wangpo. Through this virtuous act may [all beings] . . . achieve [the level of] Vajradhara, embodiment of the four Buddha bodies! May good auspices prevail!

Inscription (base plate):
Homage to the venerable Mila Shepei Dorje! May my kind mother Sonam Zemo attain Buddhahood!

密勒日巴像
衛藏，15至16世紀
銀鎏金、青銅底座鎏金，高13厘米
菩薩道收藏

密勒日巴（1040-1123年）為西藏詩人、噶舉派宗師，師承瑪爾巴。密勒日巴起初跟隨另一位上師修法，但未見受用，上師後來向他推薦瑪爾巴。瑪爾巴著其苦行，以消除往昔惡業，終授其畢生所學，而密勒日巴亦證佛果，四處遊歷說法。密勒日巴像右手支耳作傾聽狀，左手持顱杯，雙唇微張，誦唱道歌弘法。

蓮座刻文大意：

密勒日巴法王銀像，立於山峰Nyug，造像者僧人旺波。願此功德迴向眾生，願證金剛總持四身佛境！如意吉祥！

底座刻文大意：

禮敬密勒日巴！願吾母SonamZemo速證佛境！

Literature 參考書目
Weldon, D. & Singer, J. C., *The Sculptural Heritage of Tibet: Buddhist Art in the Nyingjei Lam Collection* (London: Laurence King, 1999), pl. 43.

Ricca, F., *Arte Buddhista Tibetana: Dei e Demoni dell' Himalaya* (Turin: Mondadori Electa, 2004), fig. IV.49.

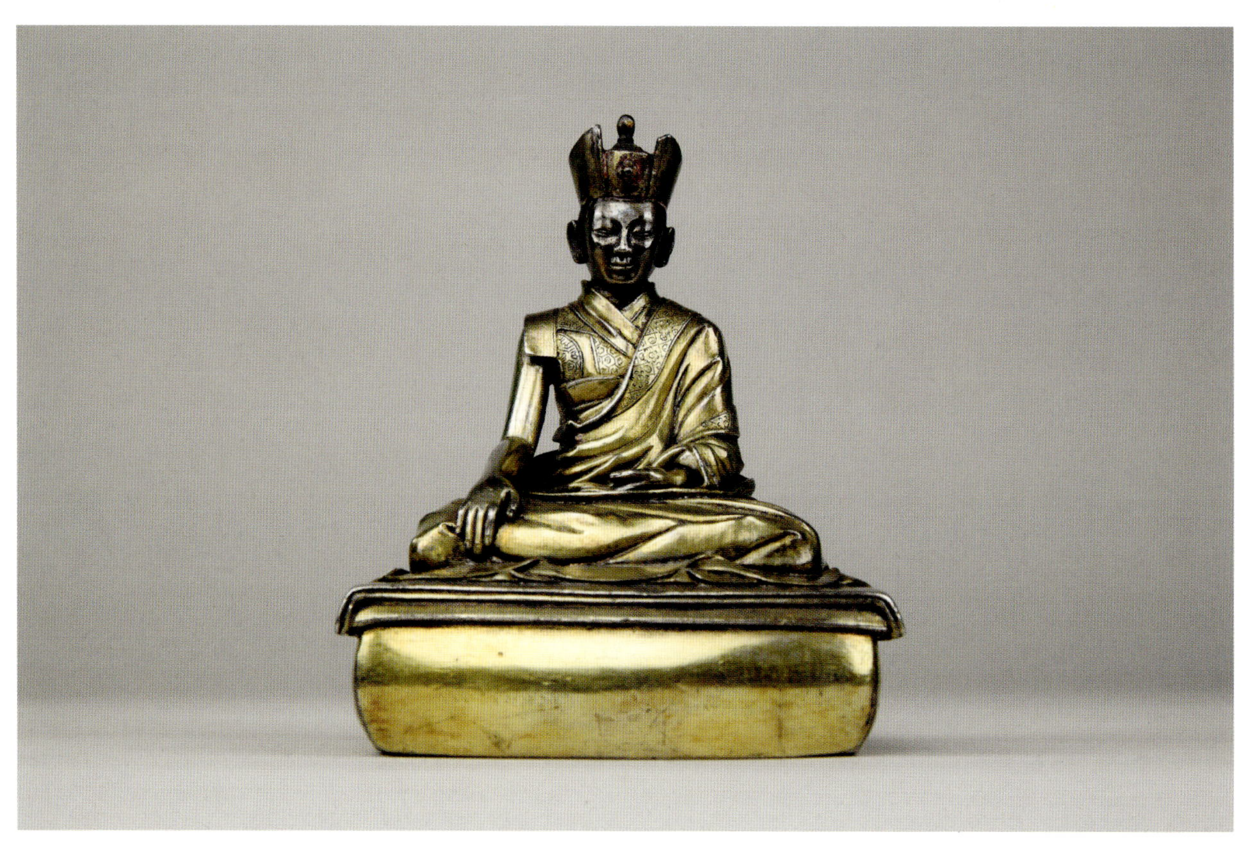

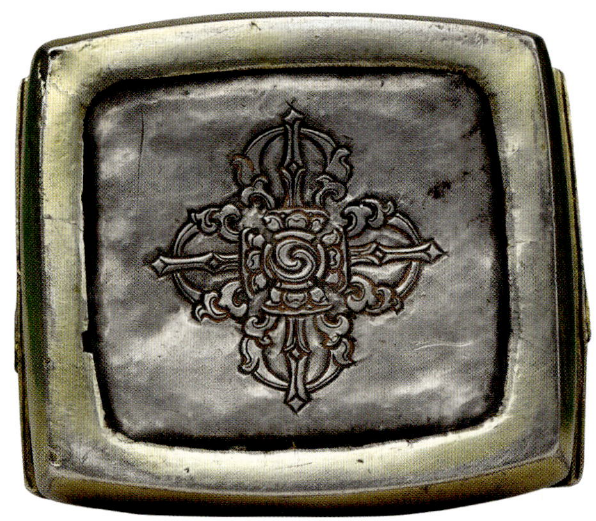

21

Figure of the Fifth Sharmapa

Tibet, 16th–17th century
Gilt silver with pigment, H. 12 cm
Private collection

Sharmapa is a lineage holder of the Karma Kagyu school of Tibetan Buddhism who is regarded as the mind manifestation of Amitabha. This gilt silver image portrays the Fifth Sharmapa, Konchok Yanglak (1525–1583), recognised as the reincarnation of the Fourth Sharmapa. The Sharmapa was formally enthroned in a ceremony conducted by the Eighth Karmapa Mikyo Dorje (1507–1554), who served as his teacher of esoteric doctrines.

五世夏瑪巴像

西藏，16至17世紀
銀鎏金、顏料，高12厘米
私人收藏

夏瑪巴是藏傳佛教噶舉派持教法王之一，該派尊為阿彌陀佛化身。此鎏金銀像為五世夏瑪巴袞秋顏拉（1525–1583年），被視為四世夏瑪巴的轉世，由八世噶瑪巴（最高持教法王，該派視為金剛總持化身）彌覺多吉（1507–1554年）主持陞座大典，並授予密法。

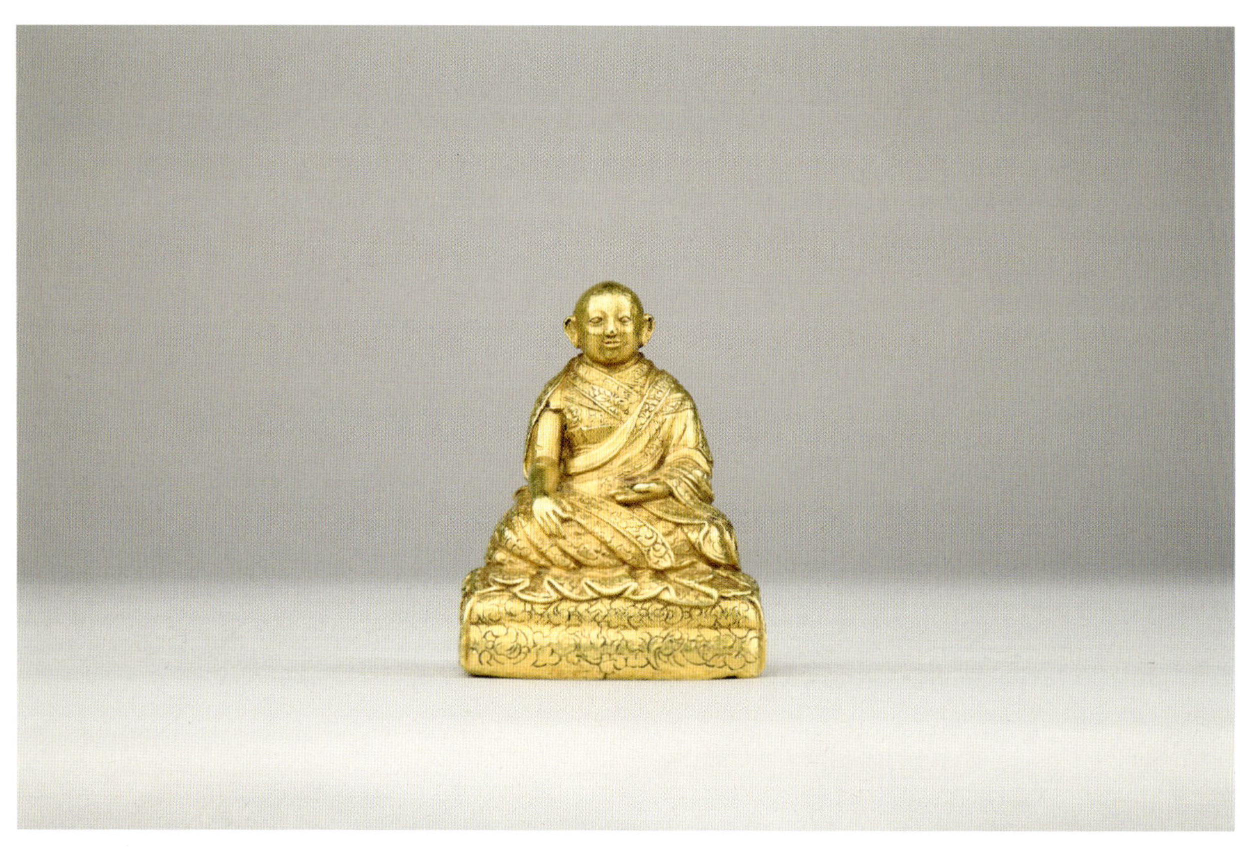

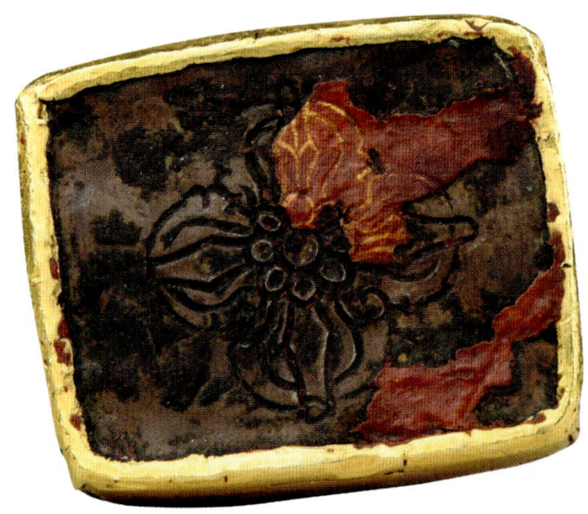

22

Figure of the Fifth Dalai Lama
Tibet, 17th century
Gold, H. 5 cm
Nyingjei Lam Collection

The Fifth Dalai Lama, Ngagwang Lobzang Gyatso (1617–1682), is also known as 'the Great Fifth'. With the aid of Sonam Chapel, his acting regent, and with the military support of Gushi Khan (founder of the Khoshut Mongols), Lobsang Gyatso was able to defeat his last political rival, the prince of Tsang, and unite all of Tibet in 1642. One of the Fifth's most famous projects was the construction of the Potala Palace as the Gelug seat of power in Lhasa.

Cast entirely in gold, this sculpture captures the Fifth Dalai Lama's stocky frame, short neck and shaved head. He is wrapped in a heavy meditation cloak with deeply incised floral scrolls, seated atop a square cushion with equally elaborate decorations.

Inscription:
The victorious king, the omniscient Ngawang Gyichuk Lobsang Gyatso, the virtuous, we honour [him].

五世達賴喇嘛
西藏，17世紀
黃金，高5厘米
菩薩道收藏

達賴喇嘛是格魯派轉世傳承的領袖。五世達賴喇嘛阿旺羅桑嘉措（1617–1682年），藏人稱為「至尊五世」。得攝政索南群培輔助，並借蒙古固始汗（和碩特汗國開國首領）之力，五世達賴於1642年推翻噶瑪政權，一統西藏。在位期間，於拉薩修建布達拉宮——此後格魯派的權力中心。

此像以純金鑄造，體態豐潤，頸項較短，頭頂光滑，僧袍飾以捲狀花紋，寶座紋飾繁多。

刻文：
尊勝王阿旺羅桑嘉措，大德，吾等禮敬。

Literature 參考書目
Brauen, M., *The Dalai Lamas – A Visual History* (Zurich: Ethnography Museum of the University of Zurich, 2005), pl. 54.

Tibet and beyond

As Tibetan Buddhism gained support from the royal court during the Yuan dynasty, numerous Himalayan artworks were brought to China, while monks and artisans frequently commuted between Tibet and China. From the thirteenth century, Chinese artistic characteristics such as flat facial features, realistic garments and the use of Chinese decorative motifs were incorporated into Tibetan statues. The Sino-Tibetan style flourished during the later Ming and Qing dynasties. Tibetan Buddhism also reached Mongolia where the Zanabazar school was popular in the seventeenth and eighteenth centuries, with statues imitating the traditional forms of northeastern India, China and Nepal.

雪域以外

元朝皇室尊崇藏傳佛教，不少喜馬拉雅珍品傳至漢土，當地僧人、工匠頻繁來往中原。故13世紀以降，部分西藏造像趨於漢化，輪廓扁平，衣紋寫實，沿用中原紋飾，明清時期漢藏藝術風格逐漸形成。藏傳佛教亦傳至蒙古，17至18世紀札納巴札爾風格盛行，其造像乃參照印度東北、漢土及尼泊爾之藝術傳統。

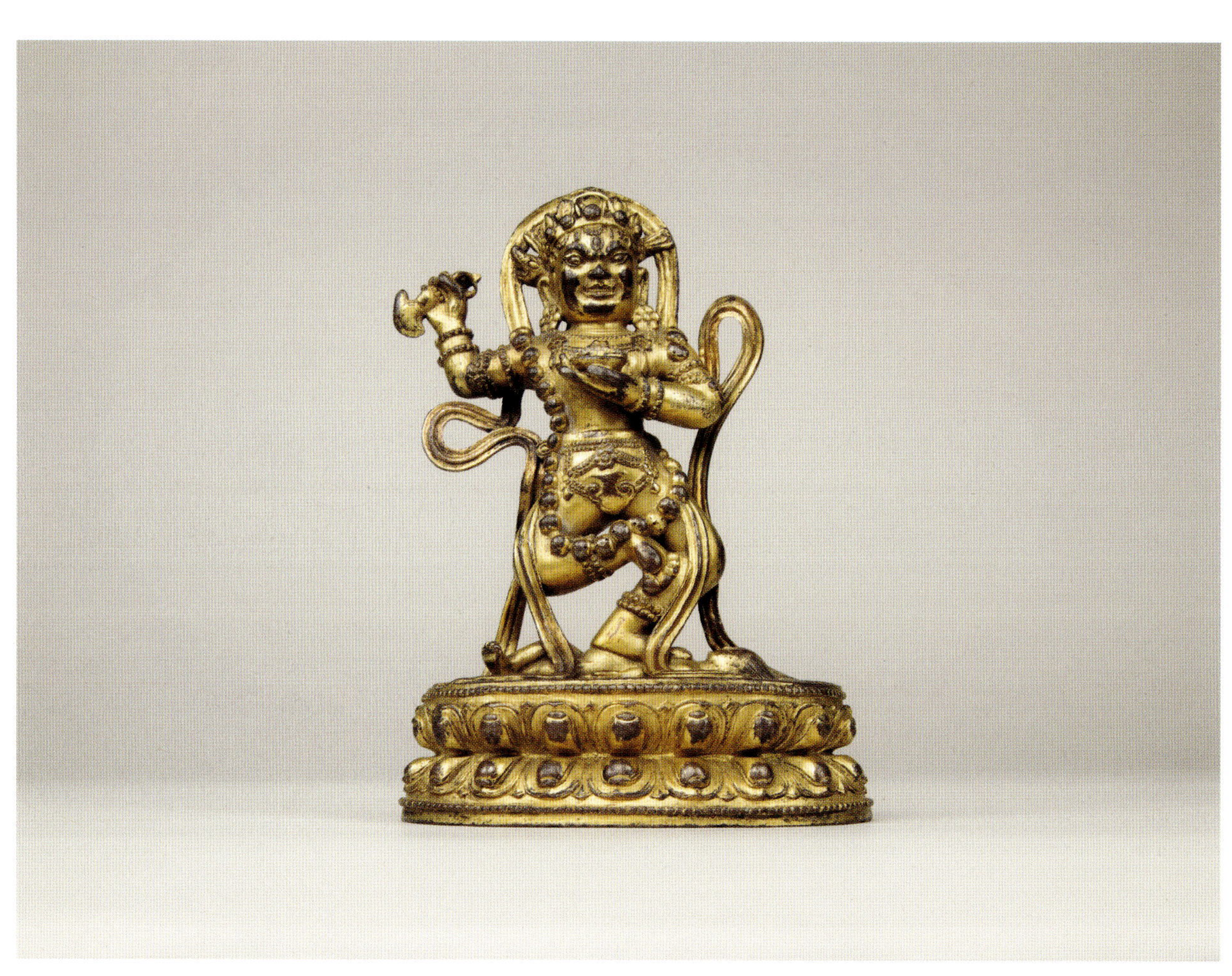

23

Figure of Vajravarahi

Yuan China, 13th–14th century
Gilt copper alloy, H. 16 cm
Nyingjei Lam Collection

The figure of Vajravarahi bares her teeth as she brandishes a *kartika* and a blood-filled skull cup. A flying sash wrapped around her silhouette draws further attention to the floral, beaded jewellery that embellishes her entire body. Stylistically, the figure's furrowed eyebrows and stockier dimensions suggest that it was made during the Yuan dynasty (1279–1368). Vajravarahi wears a cloud collar apron around her waist, a decorative motif that is commonly found on Yuan objects of varying mediums, such as ceramics.

金剛亥母像

元朝，13至14世紀
鎏金紅銅合金，高16厘米
菩薩道收藏

此像左手持盈血顱器，右手握鉞刀，帔帛擺動流暢，花蔓、珠寶裝飾滿身。體壯眉粗，為元代(1279–1368年)造像特色，裙上飾有如意雲紋，亦為當時器物如瓷器上常見的紋飾。

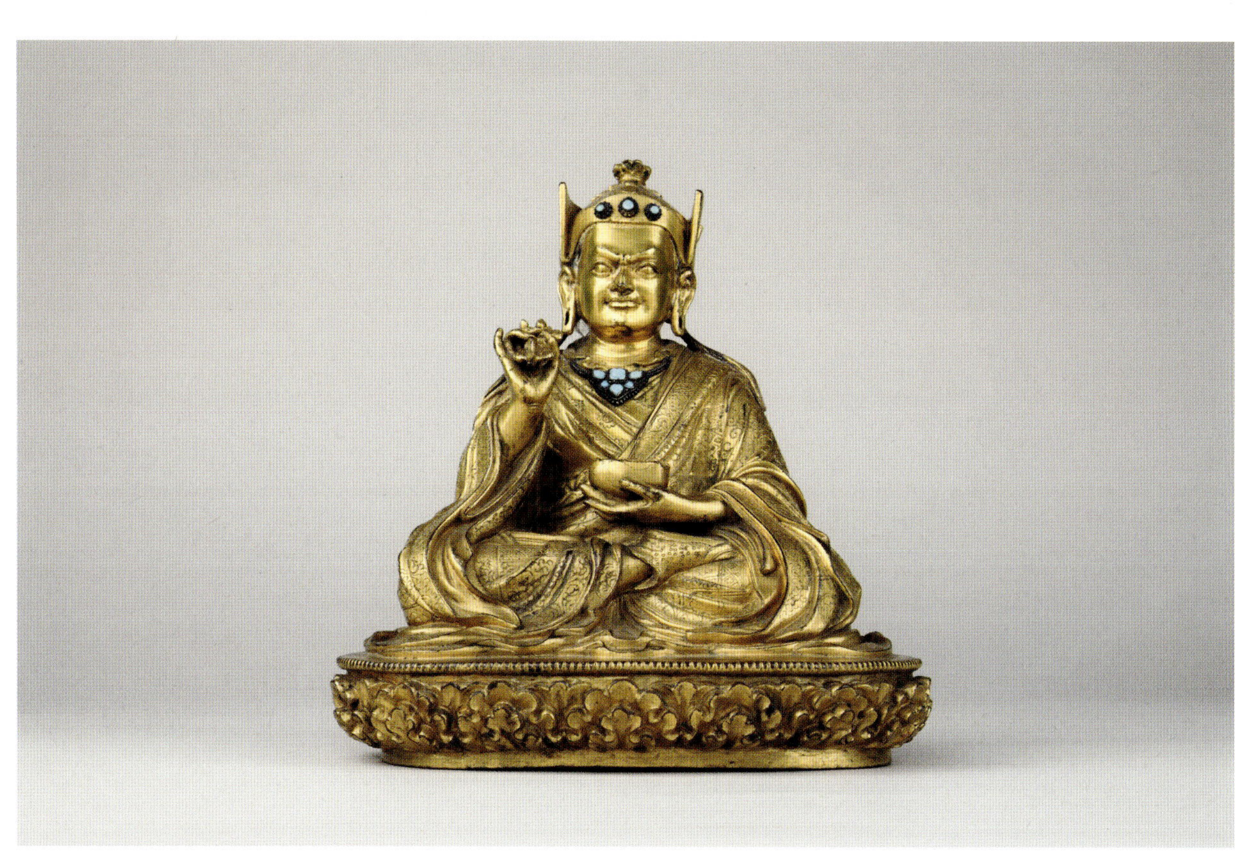

24

Figure of Padmasambhava
Tibet, 16th century
Gilt copper alloy, H. 20 cm
Cissy and Robert Tang Collection

Padmasambhava, known in Tibetan as Pemajunge (Lotus Born), is widely revered among the Vajrayana traditions as Guru Rinpoche (Precious Teacher). Also credited with the introduction of Buddhism into Tibet from India in the eighth century, he is the root guru of the Nyingma order and the 'Second Buddha' who initiated the practice of placing treasure teachings (*terma*) in hidden caches throughout the Himalayan Plateau.

Padmasambhava's face is rendered with sculptural quality and his royal attire is incised with Ming-style floral and ring-punched decorations. The crenulated lotus petals on his seat indicate Bhutan craftsmanship.

Behind the back of the lotus base are two inscriptions:
Upper inscription:

'Powerful Skull Garland [Padmasambhava], embodiment of the peaceful and wrathful sugatas. For those who in reality need to be guided by seeing the fresh air and nectar, may this [sculpture] become meaningful and a wish-fulfilling gem.'

Lower inscription:

'This wish granting image was created through pure intention, by the merit of this may Dondrub Wangyal be born in Shri Parvata, having experienced the insatiable festival of the noble doctrine of the supreme vehicle; may it bestow blessings to obtain the stage of the four kinds of Vidyadhara.'

蓮華生像
西藏，16世紀
鎏金紅銅合金，高20厘米
喜聞過齋藏

蓮花生之名意為生於蓮花，信眾尊稱為蓮師、古魯仁波切和第二佛陀。8世紀從印度入藏創立僧團，為寧瑪派之開山祖師。他於藏地埋藏許多經典，以便後世具緣弟子修習使用，是為伏藏。

蓮華生面相分明，長目高鼻，額頭寬闊，大耳下垂，長袍鏨滿錦紋，繁縟華麗，衣褶折疊自然，展現明朝造像特色。底座蓮瓣浮凸，亦顯示不丹工藝。

蓮花座後刻文大意：

上句：蓮華生為佛慈悲與忿怒相之化身。此像乃如意寶珠，助信眾得空氣（法性）與甘露（永生）。

下句：敦竹汪甲生於吉祥山，修無上乘，願供奉蓮華生，故造此像。祈願蓮師護持信眾，修持四法皆得成就。

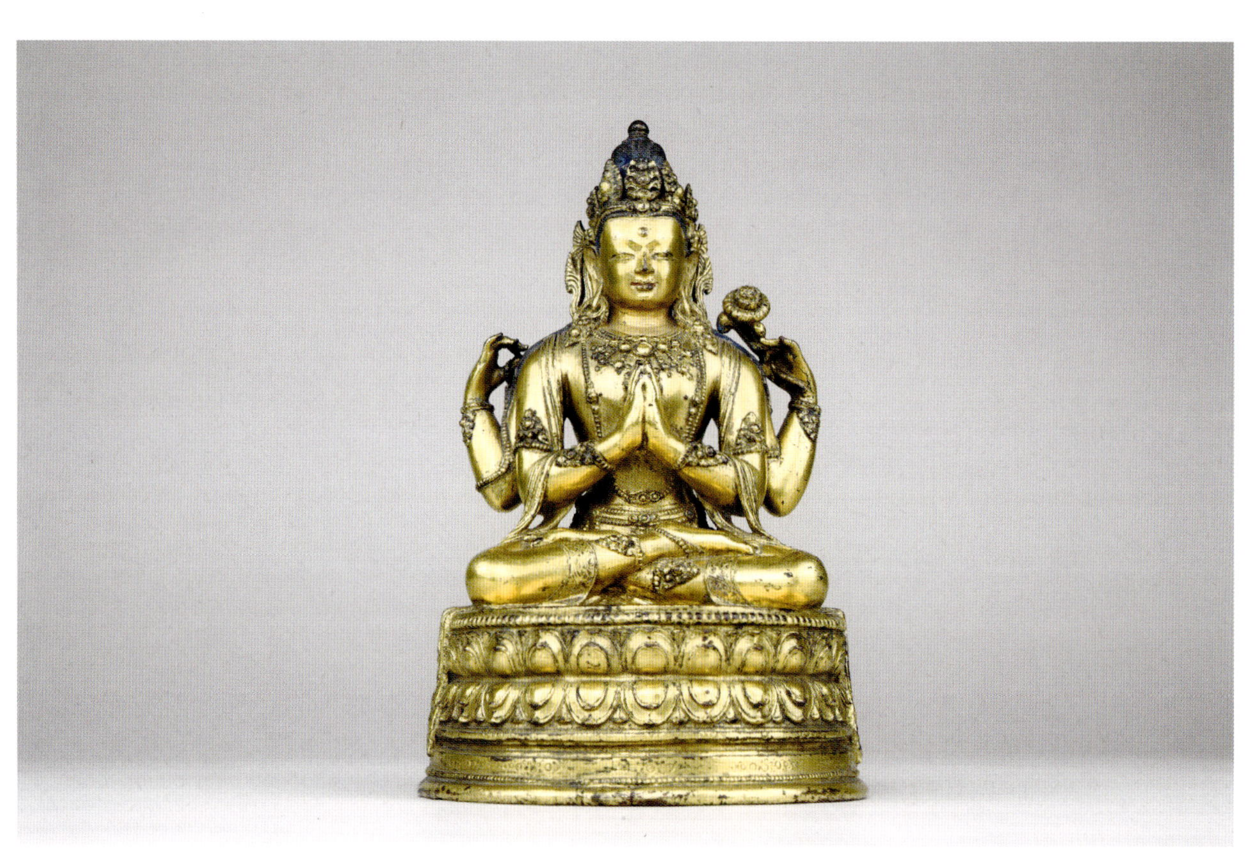

25

Figure of Shadakshari Lokeshvara

Mongolia, 17th century
Gilt copper alloy, H. 18 cm
Nyingjei Lam Collection

The Shadakshari Lokeshvara figure clasps his principal hands together in the Offering gesture (*Anjali mudra*) while gently pinching the stem of a lotus flower in his upper left hand. Here, the artist accentuates Lokeshvara's statue by adorning him with rounded jewels and draping his shoulders with a rippling sash that flows in and around his arms.

This cast image hails from the Zanabazar school. Lokeshvara has been richly gilded and modelled with a broad upper torso. The tall forehead, contoured eyebrows and pointed nose are also typical Zanabazar features, as is the enlarged treatment of the lotus petals on the base.

四臂觀音像

蒙古，17世紀
鎏金紅銅合金，高18厘米
菩薩道收藏

四臂觀音前掌合十，後方左手持蓮花。飾以瓔珞，衣緣微揚翻摺，有如漣漪。此像屬蒙古札納巴札爾風格：鎏金濃厚、身軀寬宏、額頭高闊、眼眉輪廓分明、鼻梁尖挺、蓮瓣厚實。

THANGKAS
唐卡

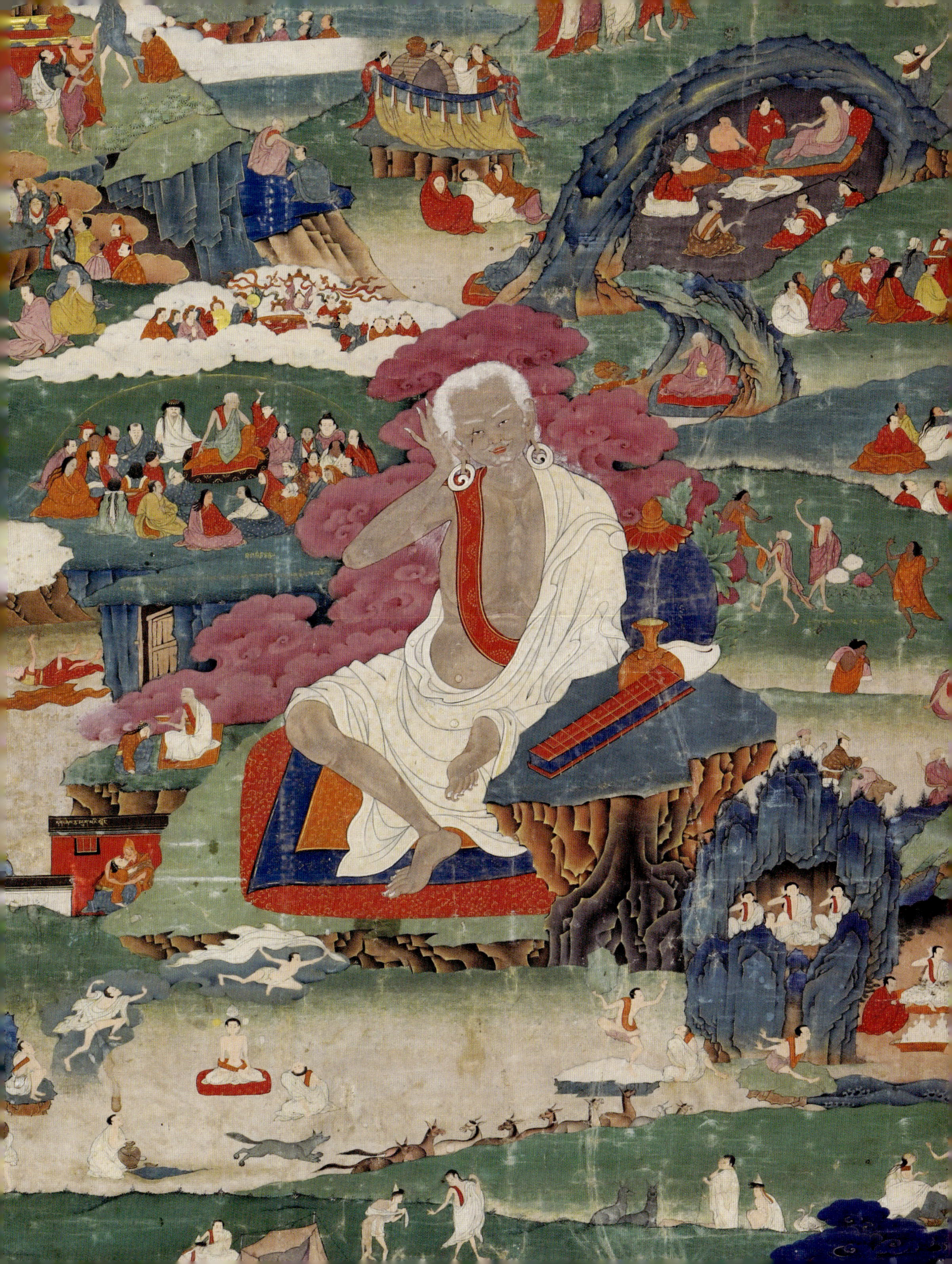

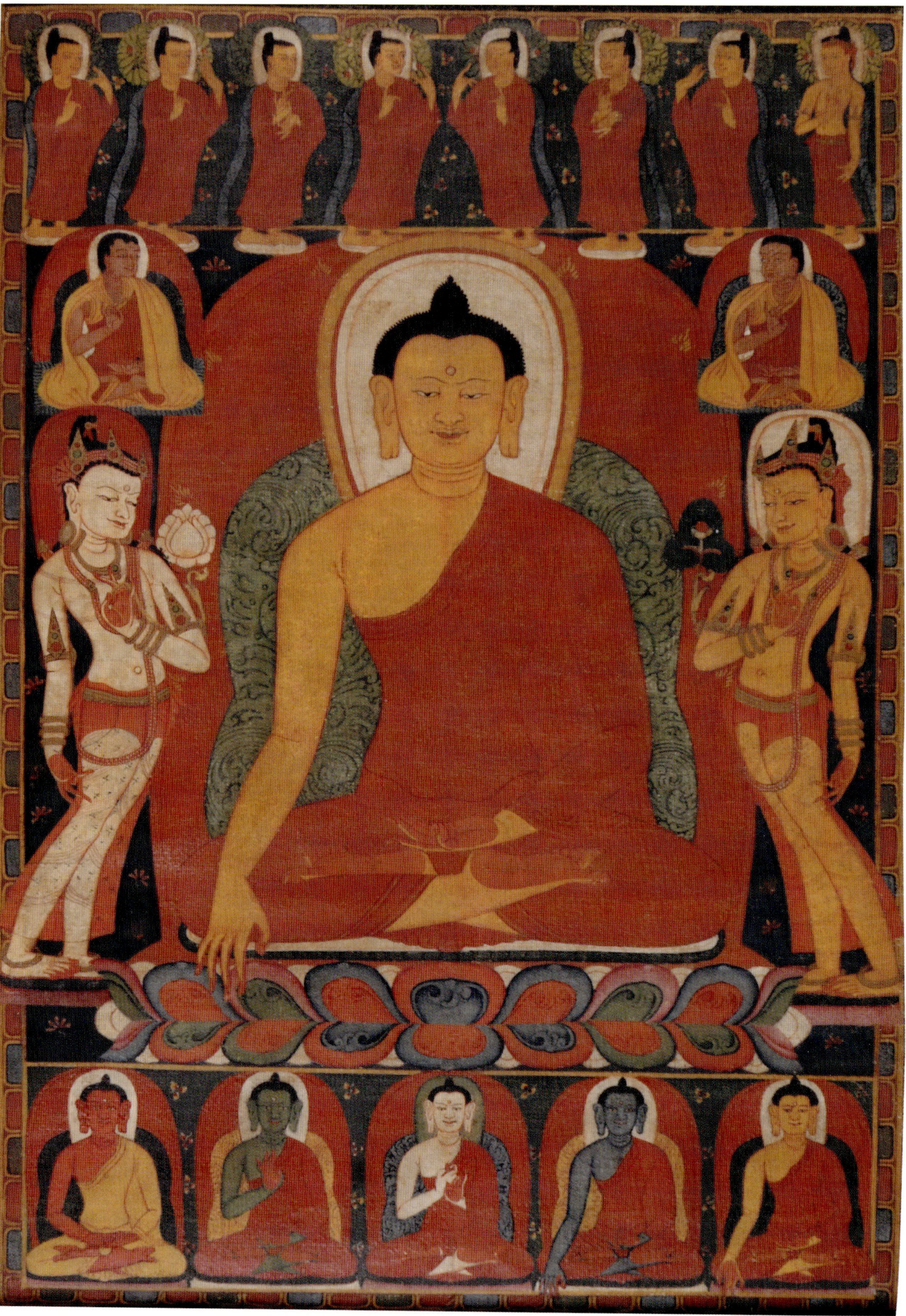

26

Thangka of Shakyamuni

Tibet, 11th century
Pigment on cloth, H. 47 x W. 32 cm
Private collection

The main image of the thangka portrays Shakyamuni flanked by two bodhisattvas—Avalokiteshvara on his right and Maitreya on the left. In the top register are the seven Buddhas of the Past and the Future Buddha, while in the bottom register are the five directional Buddhas. From the left are: Amitabha (West), Amogha-siddhi (North), Vairochana (Central) with his signature Wisdom fist (*Bodhyangi mudra*), Akshobya (East) and Ratna Sambhava (South).

On the back of the thangka is an inscription listing numerous precious objects placed in a stupa after the death of the great translator monk, Go Lotsawa Khukpa Lhetse, toward the end of the eleventh century. Khukpa Lhetse translated Indian texts into Tibetan and was likely once the owner of the thangka. However, the identities of the monk figures situated above the bodhisattvas are not mentioned in the thangka and are still debated, one of them possibly being the translator himself and his mentors.

In the eleventh-century cultural milieu, images were heavily influenced by Indian aesthetics under the Pala and Sena dynasties in eastern India and Bengal. The bodhisattvas both wear a thin and transparent garment (*dhoti*) covering the lower portion of the body over short undergarments, which was a popular form of dress in India, Nepal and Central Asia from the twelfth to fourteenth century. Some figures are painted in three-quarter profile and the foliate roundels of the scroll-work behind Shakyamuni, a motif of Bengalese—though ultimately Hellenistic—origin lived on in the Nepal Valley as part of Indian aesthetic heritage. These motifs were also adopted in Tibet.

釋迦牟尼唐卡

西藏，11世紀
棉布、顏料，高47、闊32厘米
私人收藏

釋迦牟尼由彌勒菩薩、觀世音菩薩脅侍左右。上方為過去七佛及未來佛，下方乃五方佛，從左至右是西方阿彌陀佛、北方不空成就佛、中央毗盧遮那佛（結大圓滿手印）、東方阿閦佛、南方寶生佛。

唐卡背後的文字列出藏僧譯師庫巴拉孜於11世紀末圓寂後，一佛塔中所置的諸多寶物。他從印度回藏，將眾多佛典譯成藏文，學者認為此唐卡屬庫巴拉孜。然而，菩薩上方藏僧的身分，該段文字並無所述，眾說紛紜，有說是庫巴拉孜或其導師。

11世紀，位於東印度和孟加拉的波羅和犀那王朝美學對西藏圖像影響甚大：例如菩薩下身所披的輕薄透明裹裙，流行於12至14世紀印度、尼泊爾、中亞一帶；部分人物略為側向，釋迦牟尼身後飾以捲葉紋，皆為孟加拉地區流行之圖像（原屬希臘化時期風格），源自印度美學傳統，後傳至尼泊爾河谷及西藏。

Literature 參考書目

Pal, P., *Himalayas: An Aesthetic Adventure* (Chicago: The Art Institute of Chicago, 2003), fig. 114.

Heller, A., 'Indian Style, Kashmir Style: Aesthetics of Choice in Eleventh-Century Tibet', *Orientations*, 32/10, 2001, 20–21, fig. 13.

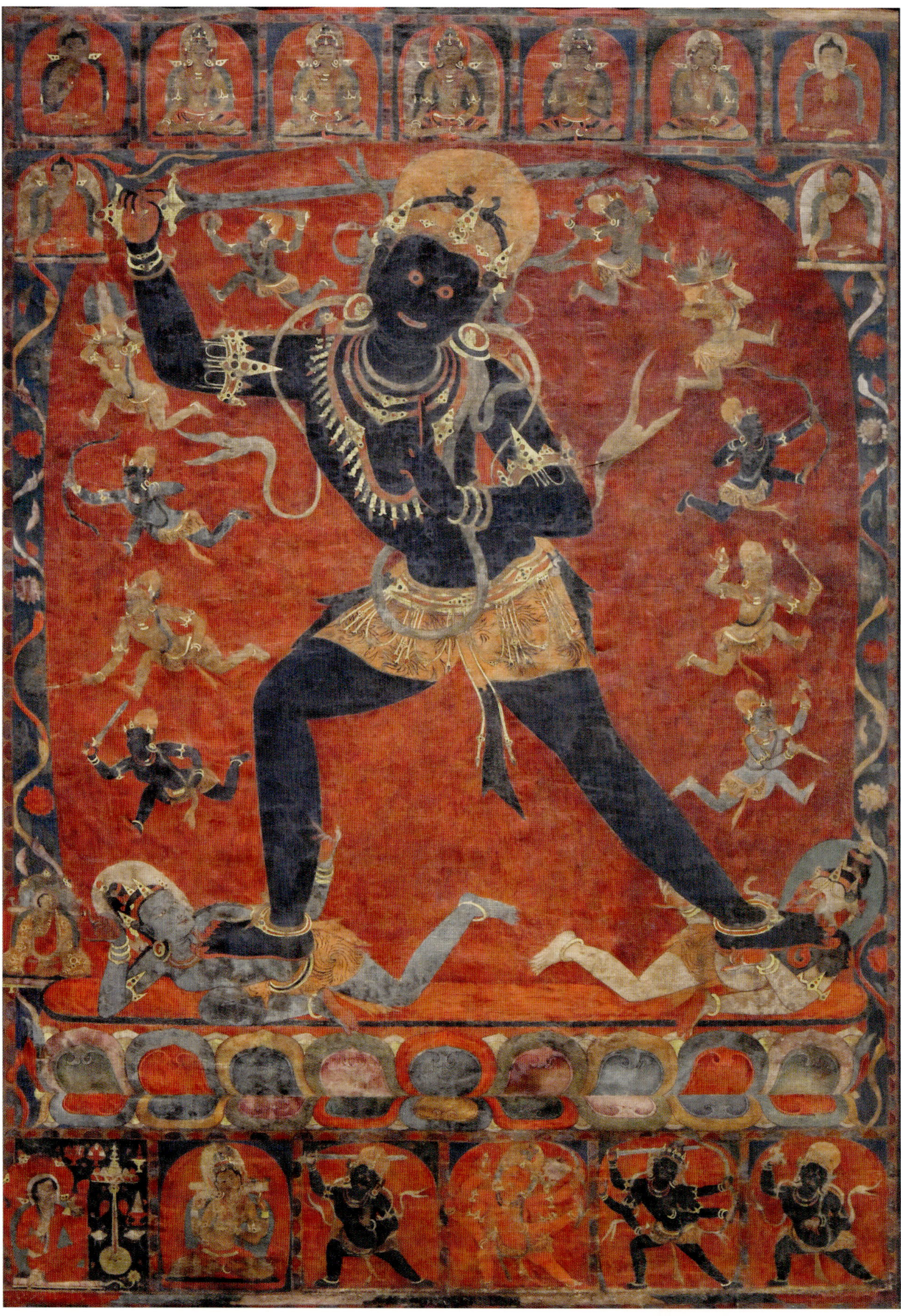

27

Thangka of Achala

India / Tibet, 11th century
Pigment on cloth, H. 116 x W. 79 cm
Private collection

Achala (The Immovable One) is one of the great wisdom kings who enables Buddhists to overcome obstacles encountered in the pursuit of enlightenment, whether the hindrance is demons causing disease or the individual's own negative mental states.

Achala stands in his characteristic warrior pose with a bent right knee, befitting his role as a guardian figure. His feet are trampling the Hindu deities Shiva and Ganesh who gaze up at Achala, here represented as *bgegs*–evil forces hindering enlightenment. Ten emanations of Achala emerge in mid-air from the main figure, each in a unique and highly animated vanquishing pose that is the outward expression of the immovable central figure's capacity to destroy all those who act improperly. Atisha, who introduced the iconography of Achala to Tibet in the eleventh century, is included at the bottom left of the main figure.

The extravagant use of gold, a Tibetan artistic feature in thangka painting, is seen in the rendering of the deity's adornments. The crowns, necklaces and belts are all composed of bejewelled golden elements supported by the red cloth.

不動明王唐卡

印度/西藏，11世紀
布帛、顏料，高116、闊79厘米
私人收藏

不動明王為佛教護法，「不動」是指慈悲不變，聞其名可斷惡修善，遠離疾苦魔障，故示以戰鬥姿態，右腿彎曲、左腿伸展，腳踏阻礙修行的魔障，唐卡中表現為印度教神祇濕婆和象頭神。身後為其十種形相，各持武器，使人斷惡修善。唐卡左下方是阿底峽大師，其於11世紀將不動明王的圖像引入西藏。西藏唐卡大量運用黃金，如不動明王的寶冠、項鍊和腰帶皆以黃金上色，並以紅布作背景襯托。

Literature 參考書目
Kossak, S., *Painted Images of Enlightenment: Early Tibetan Thankas, 1050–1450* (Mumbai: Marg Foundation, 2010), fig. 39.

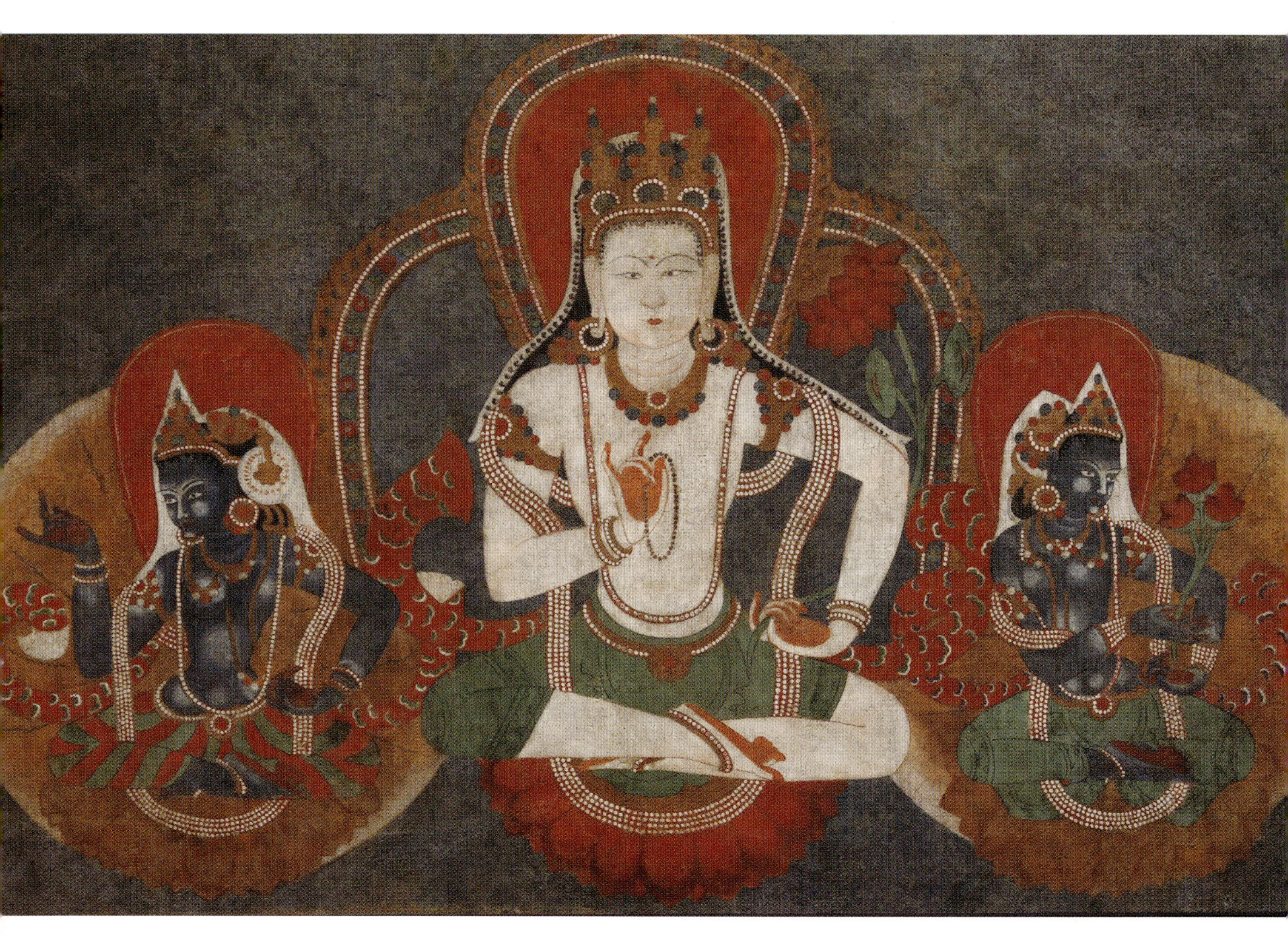

28

Thangka of Avalokiteshvara and two offering goddesses

Western Tibet, 15th century
Pigment and gold on cloth, H. 43 x W. 67 cm
Private collection

Avalokiteshvara is seated on red lotus petals in the True Sitting pose (*Sattvaparyanka asana*), his right hand holding a strand of prayer beads over his heart. His left hand is clasping the thin stalk of a deep red lotus in full bloom above his left shoulder. He wears the crown, jewellery and *dhoti* of Indian royal apparel, as well as a white cloth veil behind his crown. His head is surrounded by an ovoid red nimbus with radiant gold flames. Such representations were popular in Kashmiri art and thus inherited by the Guge kingdom in Western Tibet.

The two goddesses flanking Avalokiteshvara also have an ovoid red nimbus with a discreet gold outline, while their voluptuous blue bodies are seated on gold lotus petals within a spherical aura of gold and white. The goddess Vajrapushpa (Vajra Flower), to the left of Avalokiteshvara, has her two hands positioned to hold the long stalk of a lotus plant with three red blossoms that capture her gaze. The goddess to the right of Avalokiteshvara, Vajramala (Vajra Garland), has her left hand poised in the *vajra* fist. Both goddesses and Avalokiteshvara have their palms adorned with henna as a sacred mark of piety.

觀世音及金剛部菩薩唐卡

藏西，15世紀
布帛、顏料、黃金，高43、闊67厘米
私人收藏

觀世音結跏趺坐於紅蓮上，右手持念珠於胸前，左手執蓮花細莖，暗紅蓮花於肩上盛開。配戴冠冕、珠寶，穿上裹裙，皆為印度皇室著裝，冠冕後覆以白紗，帶火焰紋背光。此等特徵多見於喀什米爾藝術，藏西古格王國亦承襲其遺風。

隨侍觀世音左右的金剛部菩薩坐於金色蓮瓣上，帶橢圓紅色背光，外緣以金線勾勒。通體藍色，體態豐滿，坐於金色蓮花瓣上，金白色聖光環繞其身。觀世音左側為金剛華菩薩，正細看手持的三朵紅蓮。右側為金剛蔓菩薩，結金剛拳印。兩位菩薩手掌皆施彩繪，以示虔敬。

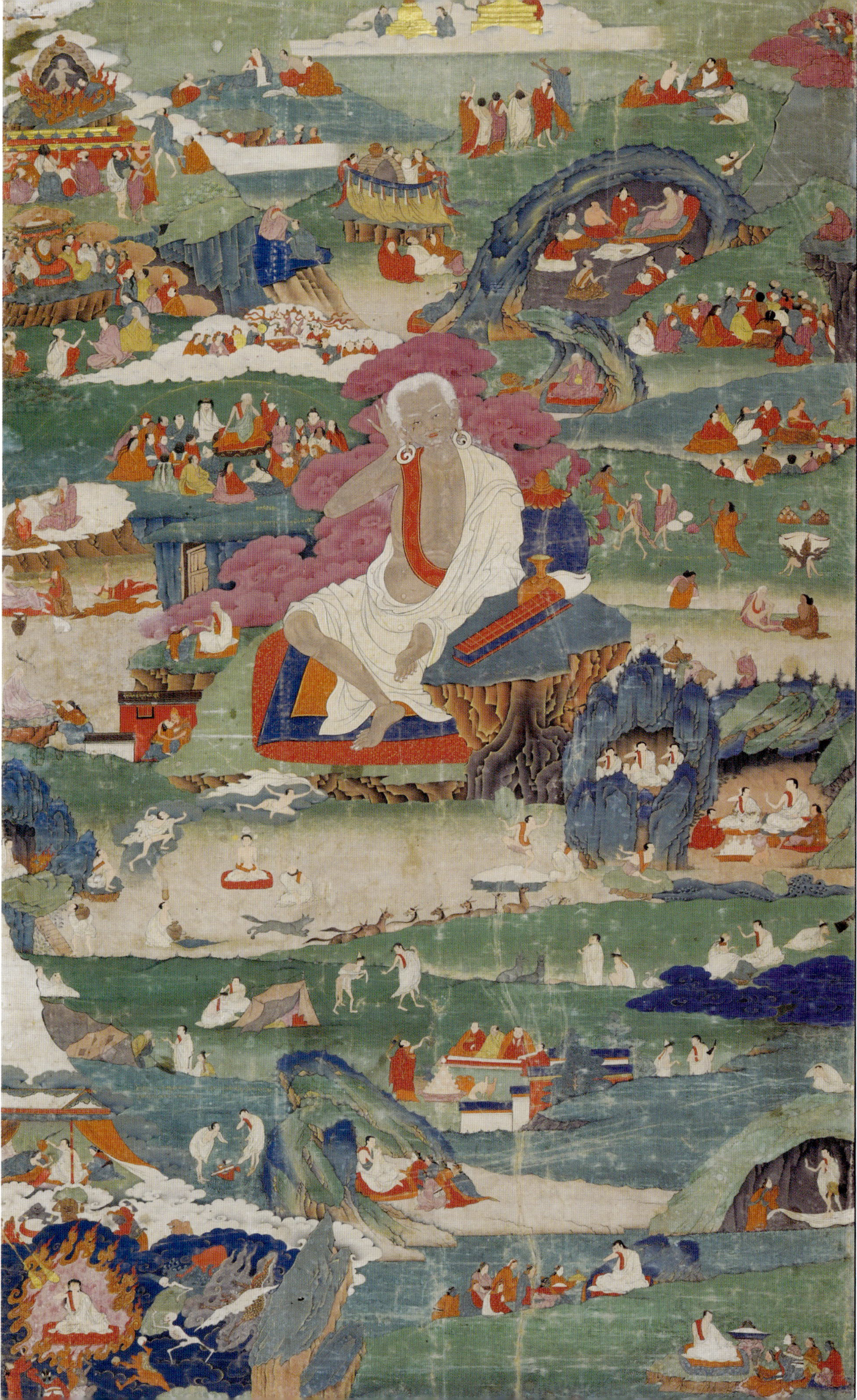

29

Thangka of Milarepa

Eastern Tibet, 18th century
Pigment on cloth, H. 108 x W. 64 cm
Nyingjei Lam Collection

The iconographic feature of the poet-saint is music. His right hand cups his right ear, or is placed near it—a gesture that singers commonly make in order to sharpen their hearing and to block out extraneous noise. He is generally portrayed with a piece of cotton loosely wrapped around an emaciated body (his name literally means cotton-clad) to indicate physical austerity and deprivation. The drooping flesh, wrinkled, ashen skin and white hair on his face and head are all indications of age. Nevertheless, the face has not lost its youthfulness, and he is in a state of reverie as he nostalgically recalls the many events of his exciting life, represented around him in extraordinary narrative details. He is depicted with a skull cup, which is placed on the rocky table beside him in the biographical painting, in which he is also given a water pot and a bound manuscript.

The thangka is a lively narrative of Milarepa's spiritual journey, as rendered in the Karma Gadri or Karma Encampment style. The Karmapas frequently travelled with large retinues that included artists. Drawing elements from Ming dynasty scrolls, the work displays the predominance of landscape elements narrating various scenes in cavalier perspectives. Although the individual natural forms may reflect Chinese motifs, the compositions and figural forms—especially the colouring with greens and blues—take precedence over the ubiquitous red of earlier styles, which reflects Tibetan tastes and mannerisms.

密勒日巴唐卡

藏東，18世紀
布帛、顏料，高108、闊64厘米
菩薩道收藏

密勒日巴是西藏以音樂聞名的行者、詩人、大成就者。他舉手兜起右耳，以阻隔雜音，專注傾聽，為西藏歌者的形象。他披單薄棉衣，凸顯枯瘦體形以及老態——肌肉鬆弛、皺紋滿佈、皮膚黯淡、白髮滿頭，更表現人身之成住壞空。然而，他面容卻精神矍鑠，皆因他正將一生經歷娓娓道來，格外雀躍。藝術表現中，他多手持顱杯，或如此唐卡般，連同水壺及束起的書卷，置於石臺之上。

此唐卡屬噶瑪嘎孜派風格。歷代噶瑪巴常四處遊歷，並有畫師隨行記錄。此風格的唐卡採用散點透視敘述不同時空，揉合山水畫之視覺元素，受明代卷軸畫之影響。儘管個別的自然形式或見諸對中國藝術主題之吸收，該唐卡的構圖、人物形象，尤其是青綠設色，則保留西藏傳統的用色，反映當地美學（早期西藏傳統風格多用紅色）。

Literature 參考書目
Pal, P., *Himalayas: An Aesthetic Adventure* (Chicago: The Art Institute of Chicago, 2003), pl. 164.

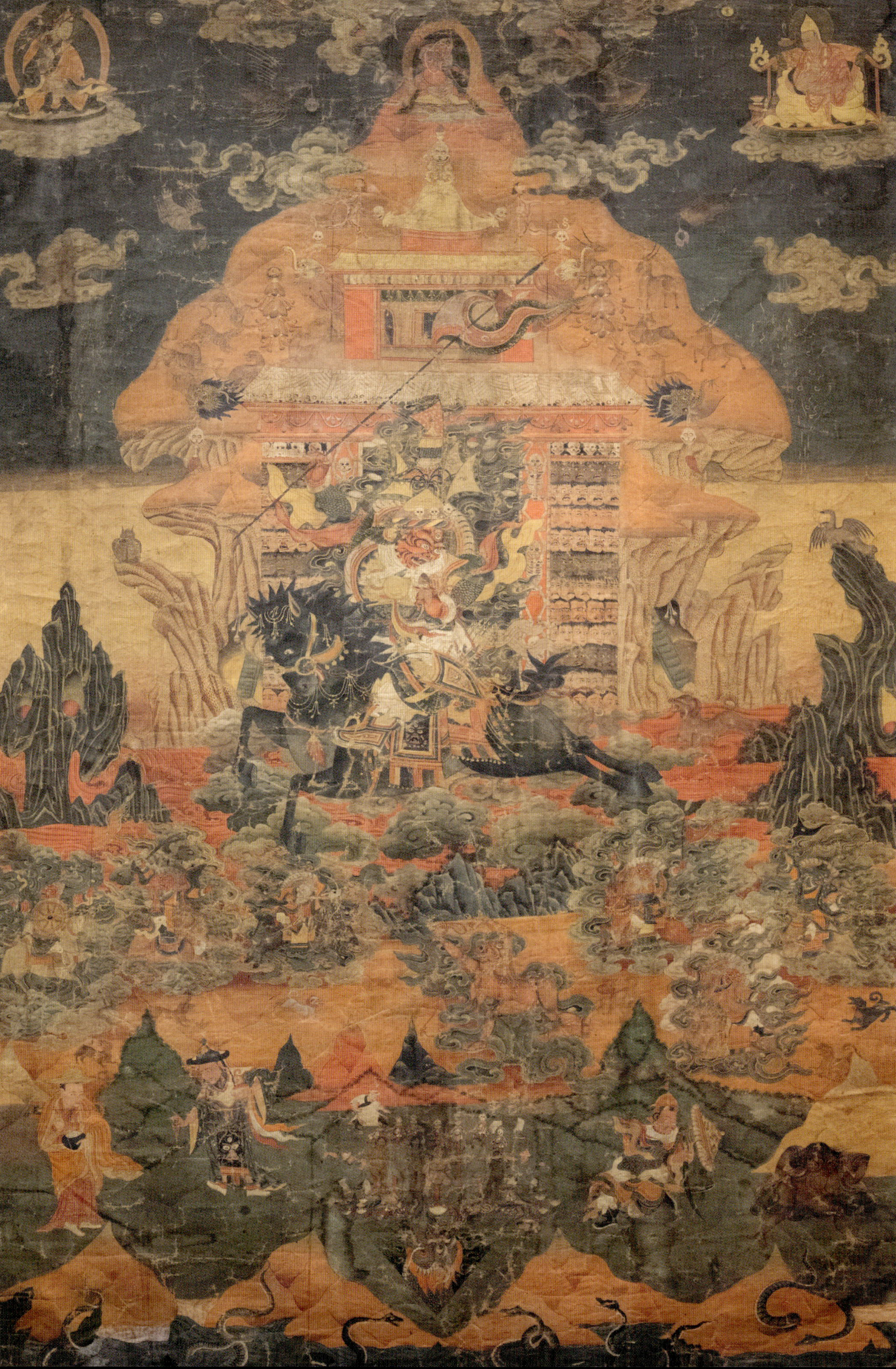

30

Thangka of Tsiu Marpo

Mongolia, 19th century
Pigment and gold on cloth, H. 117 x W. 76 cm
Nyingjei Lam Collection

Popularised by the Nyingma teacher Ngari Panchen (1487–1542), Tsiu Marpo is the tutelary deity of the Nyingma tradition of Tibetan Buddhism. He was once the head of the Seven Wild Tsen Brothers, who were later subdued by Nyingma's founder, Padmasambhava, shown here floating above a *makara*-style cloud in the painting's upper left corner, with the aid of Hayagriva standing atop the mountain. In an allusion to Tsiu Marpo's pre-Buddhist origins, the artist has emblazoned the background with a foreboding mountain scene populated by antelopes, leopards, dragons and bird demons carrying fresh corpses.

The wrathful protector strides atop a horse in a sea of blood while brandishing a spear and a cord of rope in his hands, symbolising his ability to bind negative forces. Located behind him is his palace, which has been fortified with the bones, flayed skins and severed heads of his enemies. Residing below within the charnel landscape are his six brothers on horseback accompanied by serpents, sorceresses, guardians, monks and exorcists in the process of expelling the demonic impurities from a group of men bound by wooden stakes.

紫瑪唐卡

蒙古，19世紀
布帛、顏料、黃金，高117、闊76厘米
菩薩道收藏

紫瑪為寧瑪派的護法，其法門源自於寧瑪派上師那日班千（1487–1542）。紫瑪原為贊神七兄弟之一，後寧瑪派祖師蓮華生（左上）經馬頭明王（山巔之上）所助，以神通降伏之。背景展現紫瑪成為護法前的山野場面，屢屢可見羚羊、豹、龍、鳥等魔獸叼著屍體。

紫瑪跨騎黑馬，奔馳於血海中，左手執矛，右手持勾魂索，身後宮殿掛著骷髏頭、人皮以及敵人被砍下的頭顱，顯示其降伏魔障之大威神力。下方則為紫瑪的六位兄弟，另有龍眾、僧侶、法師等，正為被縛於木柱的人驅魔。

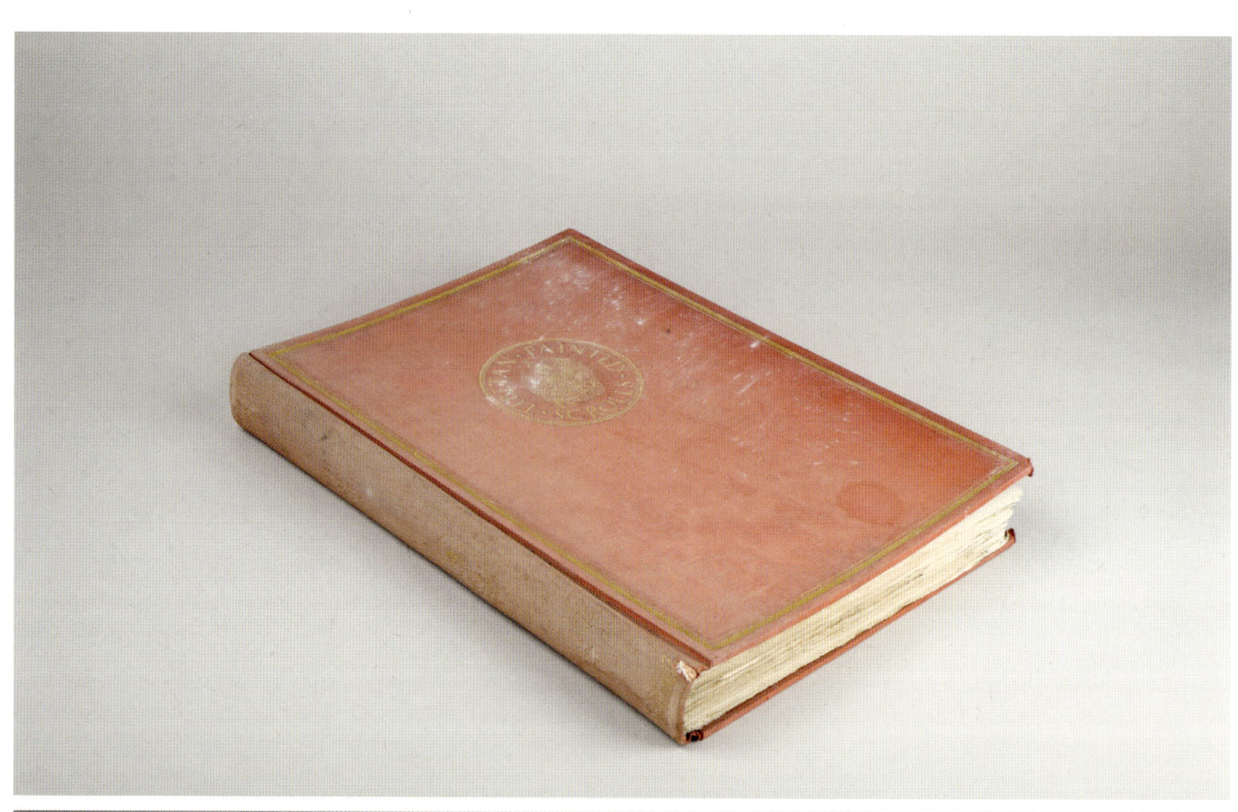

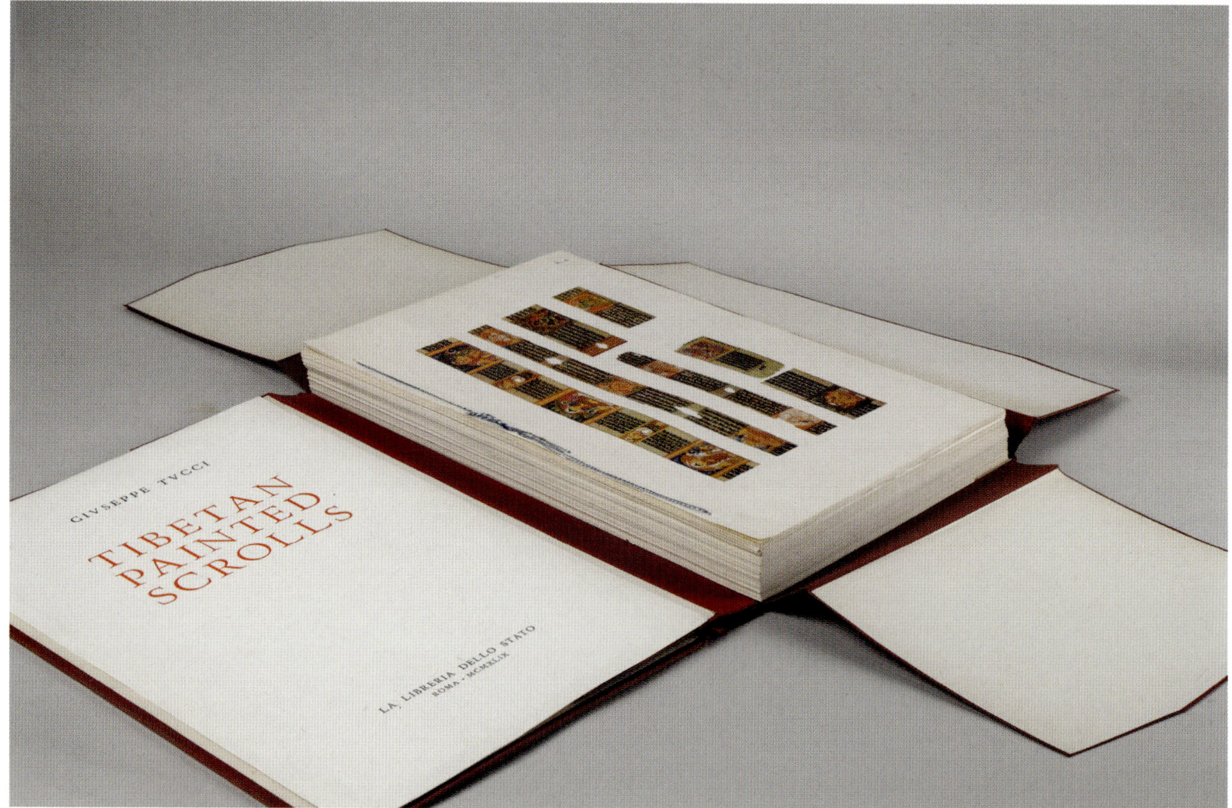
GIVSEPPE TVCCI
TIBETAN
PAINTED
SCROLLS
LA LIBRERIA DELLO STATO
ROMA · MCMXLIX

31

Tibetan painted scrolls

Giuseppe Tucci

Volumes I and II and a portfolio containing 172 plates
Number 119, la Libreria dello Stato, Rome, 1949

These books are all works by Giuseppe Tucci (1894–1984), an Italian Orientalist who specialised in Tibetan culture and the history of Buddhism. Fluent in ancient and modern languages of the East and West, he conducted archaeological excavations and surveyed Buddhist heritage in the Himalayas. He wrote extensively on the art and philosophy of Tibetan Buddhism and is considered one of the founders of modern Buddhist studies.

西藏畫卷

朱塞佩・圖齊

卷一、卷二及圖集(共172張)
序號119，羅馬國家書店，1949年

書冊為朱塞佩・圖齊(1894–1984年)所撰。圖齊是義大利東方學家，專研西藏文化及佛教歷史。精通東西古今語言，曾赴喜馬拉雅山一帶開展考古挖掘，考查佛教遺址，並撰著多部藏傳佛教藝術、思想篇籍，為現代佛學研究奠基者之一。

圖齊為現代佛學研究之先驅，對藏傳佛教藝術、文化鑽研甚深，含英咀華。

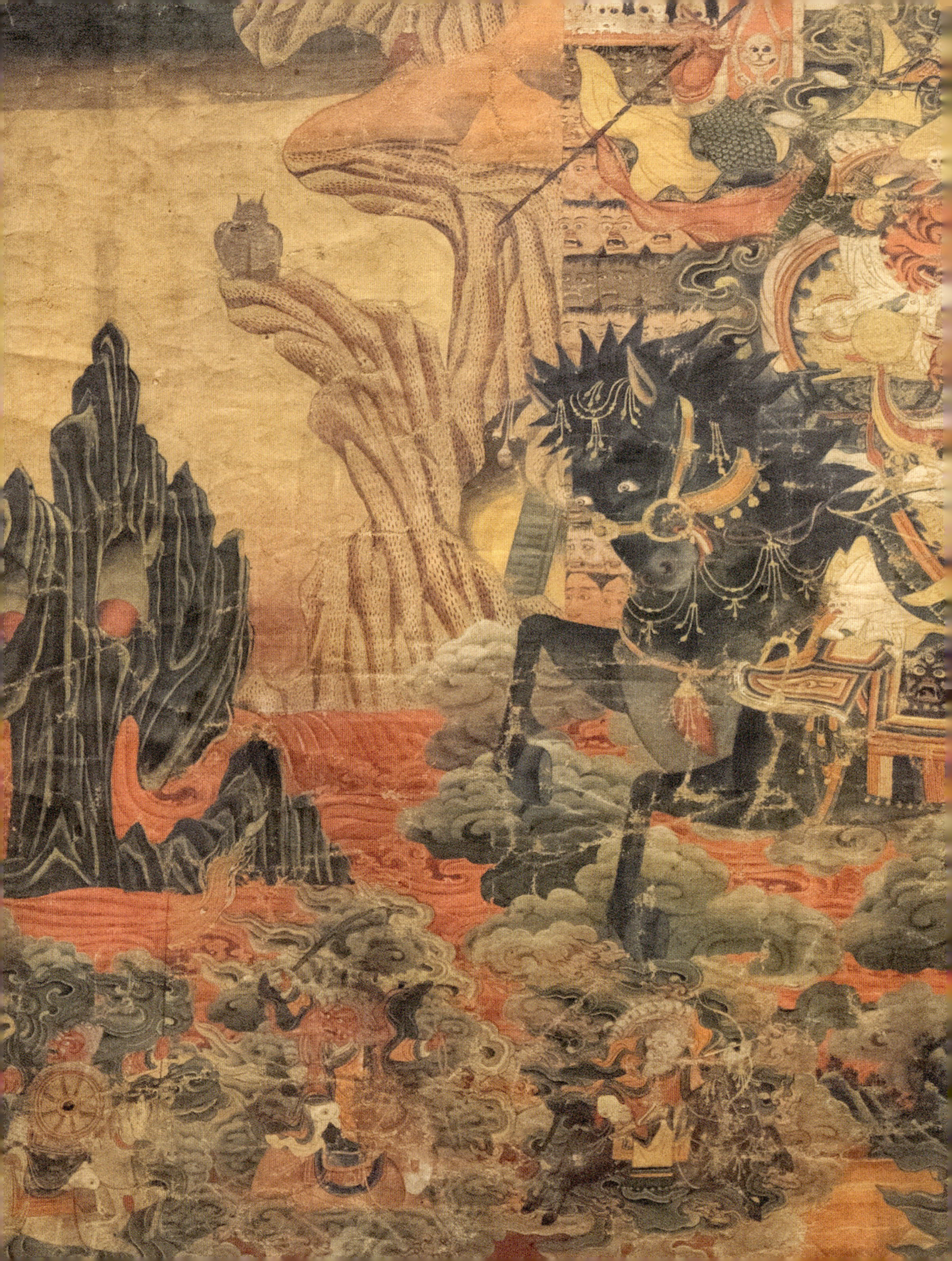

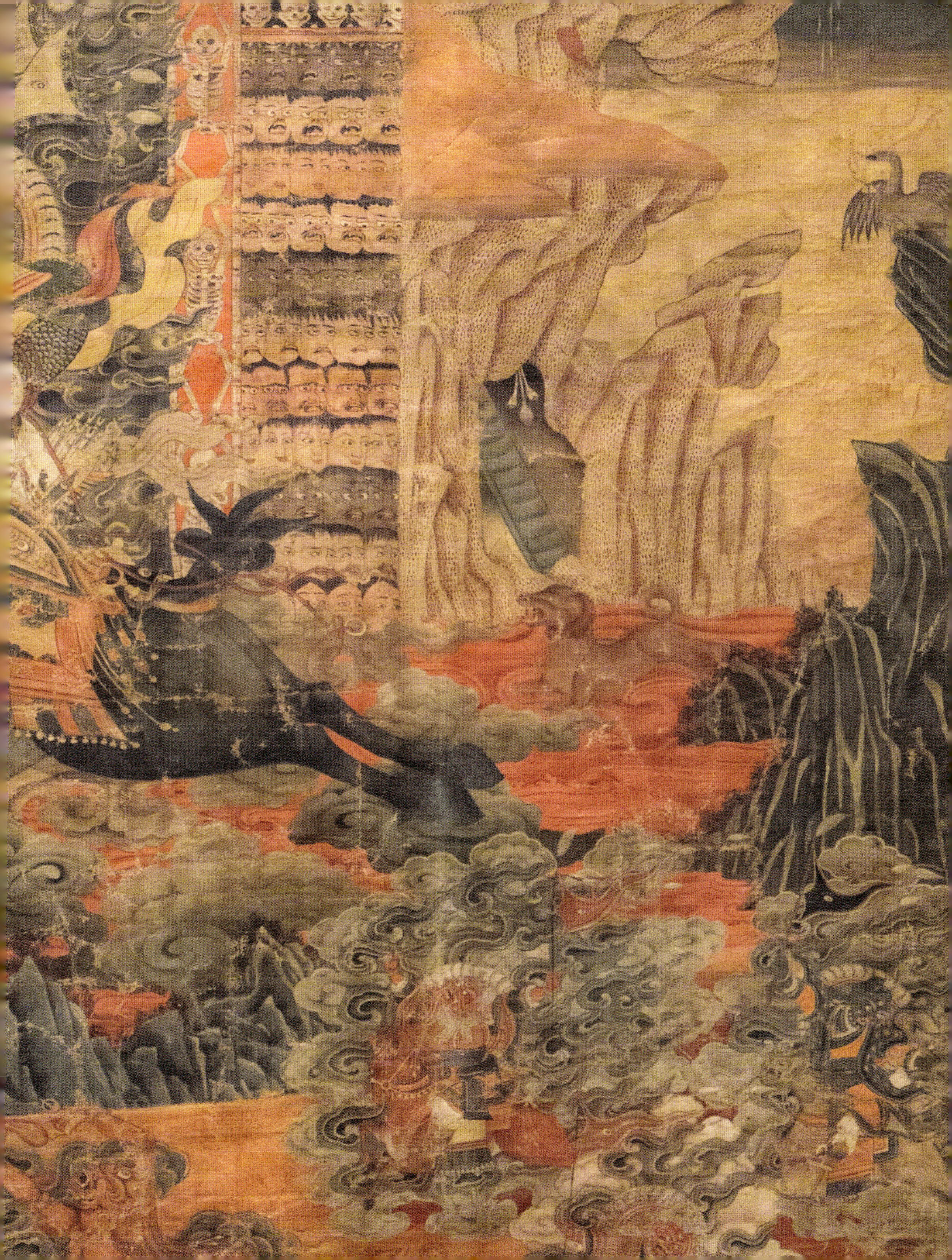

Notes on Deities in Tibetan Buddhism 藏傳佛教神祇概述

Buddha

Buddha is a title for an awakened individual who has achieved enlightenment. In Buddhism, there are various representations of the Buddha, three of which appear in this publication.

佛

佛即證道之覺者。佛教中有無量諸佛，本圖錄載錄其中三位。

Shakyamuni

Shakyamuni is the name of the historical Buddha, the originator of Buddhism. In Sanskrit, 'Shakya' is his clan name while 'muni' is the name given to a benevolent sage in ancient India. He was believed to have lived around the fifth or sixth century BCE. Born a prince of Kapilavastu (now part of Nepal), he later became a monk and at the age of 35 is said to have achieved enlightenment.

釋迦牟尼

釋迦牟尼為歷史上佛教的奠基者，釋迦是梵文族名，牟尼為古印度對聖者的尊稱。他生於公元前5至6世紀，為迦毗羅衛國（今尼泊爾）王子，後來出家，並於35歲成道。

Passed on from the Indian subcontinent to the Himalayas, Tibetan Buddhism followed the Vajrayana tradition. 'Vajra', meaning diamond, is also the thunderbolt weapon held by many deities that symbolises the immovable state of Buddha's enlightenment, while 'yana' means a vessel or vehicle. Vajrayana thus means the 'Path to Buddhahood' and its believers practice tantras and worship specific deities. Many deities in Tibetan Buddhism thus include 'vajra' in their names, and the statues are presented holding the *vajra*.

佛教傳入喜馬拉雅山一帶，承傳金剛乘教派。金剛即鑽石(金剛石)，寓意佛陀覺悟之完滿，堅不可摧，亦指法器金剛杵，象徵智慧堅利，足以斷除一切煩惱。乘是古印度一種器皿或載具，故金剛乘乃指達至覺悟的修法途徑。而藏傳佛教不少神祇具金剛之名，造像手持金剛杵。

Vajradhara

'Dhara' literally means 'Permanent Possession'. Vajradhara is the ultimate primordial Buddha and the progenitor of the Vajrayana system of Buddhism. He is represented as Sambhogakaya Buddha, one of the three forms manifested by the Buddha.

金剛總持

金剛總持是原始報身佛，代表證悟圓滿，其名有永恆統攝一切金剛之意，為金剛乘的主要神祇。

In Vajrayana Buddhism, the world is made up of five cosmic elements, which are represented through the five Celestial Buddhas. Each Buddha embodies an aspect of wisdom with a corresponding colour, cardinal direction and hand gesture. Vairochana is the central Buddha, while Akshobya, Amitabha, Ratna Sambhava and Amogha-siddhi represent the East, West, South and North, respectively.

金剛乘中，東南西北中五方，各有一佛主持，具獨特手印和顏色，分別為中央毗盧遮那佛、東方阿閦佛、西方阿彌陀佛、南方寶生佛和北方不空成就佛。

Akshobya

The 'Unshakeable One' presides over the Vajra family of Buddhas and bodhisattvas. He acts as the corrective to anger and hatred as his mirror-like wisdom reflects the world in its truest state, devoid of any distortions warped by the human ego.

阿閦佛

阿閦佛又名不動如來，金剛部諸佛菩薩之部主，具大圓鏡智，可如實照見世間事物，破除我見之愚痴。

Bodhisattvas

A bodhisattva is a person who is on the path towards 'bodhi' (awakening or Buddhahood). This refers to an enlightened being who is fully equipped to attain nirvana but has postponed it for the altruistic purpose of saving all living creatures. In order to do so, they often assume various forms, such as the wrathful ones, rendered so as to frighten away egotism—the cause of all suffering. They are also depicted in the *yab-yum* form—

the sexual union of a male and female deity, to signify the inseparability of wisdom and compassion, which is essential on the pathway to enlightenment. This publication displays two prominent bodhisattvas in Tibetan Buddhism in various emanations.

菩薩

菩薩具名菩提薩埵，菩提即覺悟、佛道，薩埵是眾生，眾生求入佛道名菩薩，並指發心度盡眾生，方入涅槃之覺者。為度眾生，菩薩現諸形相，如現忿怒相，以降伏我執，斷除苦集，又如雙身形相，即男女神祇合歡，象徵悲智雙運，以此證道。是次展覽可見藏傳佛教中兩位菩薩示現諸相。

Vajrapani

'Pani' means 'in hand', so that Vajrapani translates as the 'Vajra Holder'. As an attendant to Akshobya, he is a patron deity of Tibet, and the primary keeper of all tantric teachings. Vajrapani, Avalokiteshvara and Manjushri are the three great bodhisattvas of Tibetan Buddhism, representing the power, compassion and wisdom of the Buddha.

金剛手菩薩

金剛手，意即手持金剛杵，密法之護持者，承傳阿閦佛法脈。金剛手菩薩、觀世音菩薩和文殊菩薩並稱西藏三怙主，分別代表佛陀之力量、慈悲和智慧。

Mahachakra Vajrapani

Usually rendered in the *yab-yum* form, the male Vajrapani, symbolising compassion, embraces a female partner who represents wisdom. This signifies that only by combining the two forms can enlightenment be achieved.

大輪金剛手菩薩

大輪金剛手菩薩通常為雙身像，金剛手菩薩象徵慈悲，明妃代表智慧，是為悲智雙運。

Avalokiteshvara

Avalokiteshvara, known as Chenrezi in Tibetan, meaning 'Looking with a Merciful Eye' at sentient beings, is the Bodhisattva of Compassion. Considered to be the attendant of Amitabha, he is the patron deity of Tibet rendered in 108 emanations. All of the Dalai Lamas, the Karmapas and many other religious leaders are considered manifestations of Avalokiteshvara.

觀世音菩薩

觀世音菩薩（藏文「Chenrezig」），又稱觀自在菩薩，其名意為觀照世間音聲覺悟有情，慈悲救度眾生，為阿彌陀佛脅侍菩薩，亦為西藏三怙主之一，現108種形相。信眾奉達賴喇嘛和噶瑪巴等宗教領袖為其化身。

Padmapani

Avalokiteshvara is commonly personified as Padmapani (literally 'Lotus Bearer'), identified by the winding stem held in his left hand. The lotus is an emblem of Amitabha and is a symbol of Avalokiteshvara's immaculate purity and compassion.

蓮華手觀音

蓮華手觀音（意為手持蓮花），多以左手持蓮花莖部。蓮花為阿彌陀佛的標識，亦象徵觀世音菩薩的純潔和慈悲。

Shadakshari

Shadakshari, meaning the 'Six-syllable Mantra', is the personified form of the *om ma ni pad me hum* (hail to the jewel in the lotus) mantra, which calls upon Avalokiteshvara to help guide all beings towards enlightenment. Rendered in the tantric form with four arms, he is also referred to as the four-armed Avalokiteshvara. The four arms represent the four divine states of mind: compassion, love, sympathetic joy and equanimity.

四臂觀音

四臂觀音梵文意為六字觀音，即其心咒——六字大明咒「唵嘛呢叭咪吽」（字面意為珍寶在蓮花上），持誦此咒者，即得救度。其四臂象徵四無量心：慈、悲、喜、捨。

Amoghapasha

Another manifestation of Avalokiteshvara, Amoghapasha literally means the 'Unfailing Lasso', referring to a constant form of compassion that brings all sentient beings out of suffering and into a state of happiness leading to enlightenment.

不空羂索觀音

「羂索」為捕捉野獸的繩索，「不空」則指不落空、不遺漏。不空羂索觀音名號是指其慈悲心如羂索般，接引眾生，離苦得樂，悉皆救度，無有遺漏。

Other deity 其他神祇

Vajrayogini

Vajrayogini is the principal female deity in Tibetan Buddhism who represents wisdom. Although found in a variety of forms, including Vajravarahi in this exhibition and the female consort to Chakrasamvara, she is common to all schools of Tibetan Buddhism.

金剛瑜珈母

金剛瑜珈母是藏傳佛教重要的女神祇，為諸教派所供奉，象徵智慧，現諸種形相，如勝樂金剛的明妃及展覽中的金剛亥母。

Notes on Techniques 工藝概述

Statues

Metal has been the preferred material of Himalayan sculptors for centuries. The two primary techniques are lost wax casting and repoussé.

造像

數百年來，喜馬拉雅山脈一帶工匠多以金屬造像，其中以失蠟法鑄造和錘摞法鍛造為主。

Lost Wax Casting

Most of the smaller statues are cast using the lost wax technique. The figure is initially sculpted in wax and then carefully covered with layers of clay. Molten metal is poured in through channels to the mould's interior, which takes the place of the wax that melts and flows back out through vent holes. The various elements of a statue—the stand, pedestal, figures, arms and heads—are usually made separately and fastened together with metal clasps, dovetails or rivets.

失蠟鑄造

體積較小的造像多以失蠟法鑄造。先雕出蠟模，再覆以數層泥土。熔煉金屬後，將液態金屬倒進模具內，融化蠟模並取而代之，蠟液則經孔道流出。造像的各部分，如支架、底座、身軀、四肢、頭部等，多為個別鑄造，再以金屬扣、榫或鉚釘接駁。

Chasing

Works that are cast or created through repoussé are finished with a chisel, including the ornamental details of the clothing and plinths, as well as any facial expressions.

鏨刻

鑄造及鍛造造像最後皆經鏨刻加工，工匠以鏨刀刻劃造像衣著和底座的紋飾，以及面部輪廓。

Gilding

Many statues are gilded. An early method of gilding consisted of using a brush to apply gold mixed with resin or honey. Gilding with mercury, or fire-gilding, was later introduced to Nepal and Tibet around the tenth century. This is also known as amalgamated gilding, which involves mixing gold into a mercury solution and then placing the gold onto metal surfaces after the mercury evaporates. In Tibet and Mongolia, some metallic statues are completely painted, though generally only the face and hair are highlighted with paint.

鎏金

大部分造像皆有鎏金。早期鎏金技術是將黃金混入樹脂或蜜糖，再塗於像上。約於10世紀，汞(水銀)鍍金技術傳入尼泊爾及西藏，原理是將黃金和水銀混合，溶液塗於造像之上，待水銀揮發後，黃金即附於金屬表面。西藏和蒙古的金屬造像會於面部和頭髮鎏金，部分則通體鎏金。

Inlay

A cavity is 'hollowed out' in the metal with a chisel. The carefully cut inlays of metals or precious stones are then hammered into the parent metal. Turquoise and rubies were popular among Tibetan artisans.

鑲嵌

工匠先以鑿刀在金屬表面鑿出洞痕，金屬或寶石經仔細切割，再以錘打的方式嵌入洞內。西藏工匠喜用綠松石及紅寶石。

Thangkas

Thangkas are religious images painted onto textiles with water-soluble pigments made from ground minerals, including gold and plants mixed with a glue solution. Before and during the painting process, the artist will sometimes chant specific mantras, as well as the painting instructions.

唐卡

唐卡為宗教圖像，其顏料具水溶性，源自植物和礦物(包括黃金)，混和黏合物料後，繪於布帛上。製作唐卡之前及期間，畫師會念誦咒語和師承的繪畫要訣。

Consecration

After completion of the statue or thangka, it is consecrated with a ritual blessing by a person of high spiritual quality who invites the deity to inhabit the completed work. In some statues, sacred objects are installed within and the base is sealed. The covering of metal sheets are usually chased with an icon of crossed *vajras* that symbolise the immovable state of Buddha's enlightenment, and to fend off evil forces. For thangkas, sometimes a blessing will also include the writing of special mantras, or a high lama's handprints on the back.

開光

造像和唐卡完成後，會經高僧開光加持，祈請神祇降臨安住。部分造像經裝藏，即將聖物置於其中並封底，封板多刻有十字金剛杵，象徵佛陀修行圓滿，不可撼動，免受諸邪侵擾。而唐卡儀式有時還包括在背面寫下咒文或印上高僧的手印。